Choosing
a
College

Choosing a College

The Student's Step-by-Step Decision-Making Workbook

GORDON PORTER MILLER

COLLEGE ENTRANCE EXAMINATION BOARD, NEW YORK

In all of its book publishing activities the College Board endeavors
to present the works of authors who are well qualified to write
with authority on the subject at hand and to present accurate and
timely information. However, the opinions, interpretations, and
conclusions of the authors are their own and do not necessarily
represent those of the College Board; nothing contained herein
should be assumed to represent an official position of the College
Board or any of its members.

This publication contains material related to Federal Title IV
student aid programs. While the College Board believes that the
information contained herein is accurate and factual, this
publication has not been reviewed or approved by the U.S.
Department of Education.

Copies of this book are available from your local bookseller or may
be ordered from College Board Publications, Box 886, New York,
New York 10101.

Editorial inquiries concerning this book should be directed to
Editorial Office, The College Board, 45 Columbus Avenue, New
York, New York 10023–6992.

Copyright © 1990 by Gordon Porter Miller. All rights reserved.

The College Board, Scholastic Aptitude Test, SAT, and the acorn
logo are registered trademarks of the College Entrance
Examination Board.

Library of Congress Catalog Number: 89-081650

ISBN: 0–87447–333–0

Printed in the United States of America

Contents

Chapter 1: College Choice ... Tough Choice ...
Your Choice   1

Chapter 2: What Decision Making Is All About   11

Chapter 3: Accepting the Challenge—
Taking Charge   25

Chapter 4: Building a Solid Foundation
for Your Choice   31

Chapter 5: Looking Around:
Getting Beyond the Obvious   55

Chapter 6: Looking Around:
Getting Creative   65

Chapter 7: Using Information as Power   83

Chapter 8: Looking Ahead:
Narrowing the Field   97

Chapter 9: Selecting What's Best for You   111

Chapter 10: Applying for Admission
and Financial Aid   123

Chapter 11: They Decide, You Decide   139

Chapter 12: When Things Don't Work Out   149

Chapter 13: Stepping into Your Future
—The Opportunity   155

Resources and References   159

Index   163

College Choice . . .
Tough Choice . . .
Your Choice

L ife is full of decisions, and the college choice is one of the most important and difficult. It is important because it can have significant impact on your future, and it is difficult because it will be based upon special needs and wants that you may not be very sure about at this stage of your life. Sometimes people drag their feet when faced with important and difficult decisions. Rather than face their anxieties, they delay with the hope things will fall magically into place. There is no magic to choosing a college. It involves time, effort, and a great deal of energy. Above all it requires knowing yourself.

The purpose of this book is to help you make the right choice so you can get the very best from your future. It is a book to teach you how to go about deciding so you'll have a good chance of getting the results you want from your college experience. To approach this choice without a clear sense of how to make a well-considered decision is to ask for trouble. To delay the decision and hope for the best will guarantee disappointment. To cop out and to allow others to make the decision for you will most probably mean your needs, priorities, and dreams will not be met.

A number of factors get in the way of making a sound college choice. One of these is the difficulty of deciding about your future when it appears so distant and vague. After all, how can you make a choice about college when you have little or no idea of what you want to do in your life? Another force having an impact on your decision will be other people. Your parents will have ideas about where you should go to college, as will your friends, teachers, and counselors. In fact, they may be a lot more certain about where you should go than you are! Still another reason for having trouble with this decision is what might be called "overchoice"—you will have to choose between dozens and dozens of institutions that look so similar it appears impossible to make any real distinctions among them. The sheer amount of information gathering required to make this decision can be exhausting as well. It's especially difficult to get down to some thorough research when so many things are going on in your senior year—things with far more appeal than the completion of an application to college!

Your biggest challenge in making this decision will be to come to grips with the things that are important to you now and that you expect to be important to you in the future, things that you want the college of your choice to accommodate. This means that you'll need to spend a good deal of time thinking about yourself and what is important to you and why.

You can begin to see why the college choice is not easy. On the flip side, it is a real opportunity to define the next few years of your life in terms of where you want to be, with whom you want to spend your time, how you'll spend your time, and what outcomes or results you want to get from this very special experience. There will be very few times in your life when you'll have such an opportunity to design the specifics of what you want the future to be. That's precisely why you'll want to give your best effort to making this decision.

This book has been developed so you can get the best of the future. It features a straightforward step-by-step decision process that can be applied to any important choice. Specifically, it will help you come up with the highest quality decision possible.

When it comes to choosing a college you are faced with a two-stage decision. The first deals with the question, Which colleges are most suitable for me? From this group you will pick the colleges to which you will apply. The second stage takes place after you are offered admission by colleges. At this point you'll have to decide where you will enroll. This book gives you a tried and tested process for addressing both of these decisions. It is organized so you can work through a variety of questions, self-study inventories, and exercises that will enable you to use what you know to get what you want from your college choice. It won't be easy at times, but as you go along you're actually going to enjoy the experience!

Thought Starter

What's your favorite college?
What are you most looking forward to about college?
What could prevent you from making a good decision?

What the College Choice Is and Is Not

You'll hear a lot of stories about how people decide which college they will attend. Some go because of friends, others like the atmosphere they feel when they visit, some go on the advice of a guidance counselor, and some may even flip a coin! In any case, there's a great deal of mythology, overreaction, anxiety, and ignorance attached to making this choice. Let's take a look at what the college choice is and is not.

The College Choice Is

Difficult

Important

Normally the prime responsibility of the student

Time-consuming

Frustrating

Apt to have long-term consequences

Important to others besides the student decider

Something requiring help from others

Resolved through coming to grips with personal priorities and goals

To be reexamined periodically as changes in the individual and/ or college occur

Based on facts and feelings

The College Choice Is Not

Final

Irreversible

A guarantee for future success

A matter of luck

Static (unchanging)

The most difficult decision you'll make in your life

For others to make for you

The same for any two people

To be made in isolation

In sum, the choice is yours and so is the responsibility. It is important, but not without some escape opportunities. Furthermore, it's a choice that is difficult to make in isolation because of the many external factors that will or could have an impact on your decision.

4

Who and What Influence Your Choices?

In order to make the best decision for yourself, it is important first to identify and understand those things that might affect your attempt to make this decision. Think of these factors as *influencers*, or things that might move you in one direction or another. A good way to begin identifying your influencers is to imagine that you are in the middle of a decision and surrounded by some common influence factors.

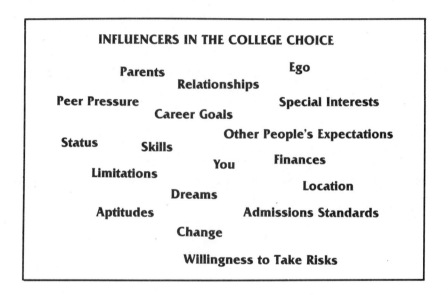

INFLUENCERS IN THE COLLEGE CHOICE

Parents　　　　　　　　Ego

Relationships

Peer Pressure　　　　　　Special Interests

Career Goals

Other People's Expectations

Status　　Skills

You　　Finances

Limitations

Location

Dreams

Aptitudes　　Admissions Standards

Change

Willingness to Take Risks

Look at the illustration above and think about your own situation. Take a moment and circle those influencers that you are already aware of. Are there additional influencers you've encountered? Add them to the illustration. Then, put an asterisk next to the top five influencers you expect you'll have to deal with in your choice. Be aware of these influencers as you go through the rest of this book.

Make a list of all of the decisions that affect you in the following ways:

1. Decisions that are almost automatic, requiring little thought

   _____

   _____

2. Decisions I always ask for adult advice about _____

   _____

   _____

3. Decisions I make only after consulting with close friends

   _____

   _____

   _____

4. Decisions I usually try to avoid _____

   _____

   _____

5. Decisions I don't care about _____

   _____

   _____

6. Decisions I spend the most time on _____

   _____

   _____

   _____

Now you are a little more aware of yourself in relation to the decision process—which influencers might affect your decision and how you respond to making different types of decisions. Let's do one more useful exercise before moving on to your introduction to the decision process.

Write down answers to the following questions as best you can. If the question is premature or irrelevant in some way, simply skip to the next one. Be as *specific* as you can in your responses.

What are three things you want most from your college experience?

1. _____

2. _____

3. _____

What kinds of pressures from others are you feeling right now regarding your college choice?

_____

_____

_____

What's your biggest worry about attending college?

_____

_____

_____

_____

How far from home would you be willing to travel?

_____

_____

_____

What are three things you'd like the college of your choice to offer?

1. _____

2. _____

3. _____

Looking at yourself both in school and out, what are the assets that will help you succeed in college?

_____

_____

_____

Who or what will be your most helpful resource in making your decision?

_____

_____

_____

What is your number one reason for going to college?

_____

_____

_____

Why do your parents want you to go to college?

_____

_____

_____

Is there anything that might prevent you from attending college immediately after graduation from high school?

_____

_____

What will a "successful college experience" mean to you?

_____

_____

_____

Whether you found these questions easy or difficult doesn't matter. What does matter is that questions like these are going to require your full attention as you begin to tackle the college choice. As you work through a series of activities in the next chapter, which is all about how to make difficult decisions, you'll have an opportunity to refer back to the three exercises you have just completed. Along the way, you may want to enlarge upon or change your initial responses.

Thought Starter

Why is going to college full-time a better choice for you than getting a job and going to college part-time?

CHAPTER

2

What Decision Making Is All About

The future does come down on you pretty fast, and the decision you make about college is a big step into that future. The future of your dreams won't just happen; it's very unlikely that things will fall into place by chance. The long-time lesson of history—and it applies to individuals, organizations, and civilizations—is that planning is the best way to get the results you want. Since a plan can be defined as a set of decisions made today that will have an impact on the future, our first concern is to make decisions of the highest quality. That is precisely what the rest of this book is all about.

What Is a Decision?

First of all, a decision assumes you have some options to choose from. If, for some reason, you're permitted to attend only one college there is no decision involved. On the other hand, you do have a choice if you are permitted to decide between the one college and not going to college at all.

This brings up an important point. While this book is to help you make a decision in terms of choosing the best college for you, you will benefit from the activities even if you are undecided or don't plan to attend college immediately after high school. In fact, you may find it will reinforce your choice or help to clarify your reasons for not attending college at all.

Second, a decision is an action and nothing more. Finally, in order to act or take action, you will have to commit your resources to the course of action. If you decide to go to college, you will have to commit your time, money, and other resources to school.

In defining *decision*, then, the key words are *choice*, *action*, and *commitment* of resources to the action or choice. The overall objective is to commit your precious and limited resources to the course of action that will yield the most desirable results.

The flip side of making a decision is that when you choose or commit yourself to one thing, you're going to have to give something up. If you go away to school you may have to give up things you've taken for granted, such as having somebody to do your laundry, home cooking, easy access to a well-stocked refrigerator, the privacy of your own room, and so forth. Not that you can't live without these niceties, it's just that some or most of them may not exist in the typical college dorm!

Now, you might give up something for an alternative you think will be better, but what if it doesn't turn out that way? Remember, you're making decisions today that will have an impact on your future, but—and it's a big "but"—there is no guarantee you'll get the results you want even when you make the best possible decision. That's because you can't control the future, and the future is where the outcomes of your decisions will take place. That's the bad news—there is no guarantee. The good news is you have a much greater chance of getting what you want if you make an informed decision. By converting your decisions into an action plan for the future, you get another bonus—you'll reduce your chance of being devastated or surprised. As a skillful decision maker you will have identified those results you don't want and you will have learned how to respond to them should they occur.

Four Critical Decision Stages

The high-quality decision involves four basic stages or phases, which are summarized below. Each stage and its required action steps will be explored in detail later, as you apply each directly to your college choice.

Stage 1:   *Identification*
This stage involves taking a look at the past and the present. At this stage, you will define your decision and look ahead to some of the results or outcomes you want. The action steps will help you to get a firm and clear grasp of the things that are important to you now or might be in the future.

Stage 2:   *Alternative Development*
At this stage, you will learn how to open up your mind; to look beyond the obvious. You will use the priorities you develop in Stage 1 to explore new options.

Stage 3:   *Selection*
Here you will compare your options and their potential outcomes. You will examine the kinds of risks you're willing to take, and you will develop your own risk-taking strategy for selecting your number one option. Much of the work done at this stage will be to evaluate information and fill in any information gaps.

Stage 4:   *Action and Control*
At this stage, you will work through steps that

Stage 4
(continued) will help you write applications for admission and financial aid. You'll learn how to monitor the progress of your decision and applications and how to plan for the unexpected. In addition, you'll learn how to predict what might happen if your first choice turns out to be a disappointment after you have made a commitment to it.

The above stages describe some of the prerequisites for making a well-informed, well-considered decision. Shortly, we'll explode these stages into 10 critical decision steps, and you'll walk through each step as it relates to your college choice.

Decision History and Self-Exploration

Before you move on to the 10 decision steps, take some time to work through the following four exercises. They will help you discover or clarify some things about yourself and your decision-making history that will be useful to know as you begin the decision-making process.

Thought Starter

Think back over the last three to five years and identify the most significant events you can remember. What good and bad things did you learn from these events?

EXERCISE 1. Your Best and Worst Decisions

Take a moment and think about some of the decisions you have made up to this point in your life. Now identify what you consider to be an example of one of your best and one of your worst decisions.

My best decision: _____

_____

_____

My worst decision: _____

_____

_____

Once you have identified each, go back and jot down why you think each turned out the way it did. To help your thinking along, ask yourself how you made each decision. Did you do it because

Everybody else was doing it?

There didn't seem to be another choice?

You had thought about what you wanted carefully before deciding?

Somebody said you had to?

You had done a lot of research and advance planning?

You had a feeling or hunch it would turn out to be the best?

As you can see, there are lots of ways of making decisions and they all begin with the same person—you!

EXERCISE 2. Decision History and Future Choices

In this exercise you have an opportunity to sketch out your decision history and some of the decisions you expect to face in the future. Write down one to three decisions that you made five years ago, three years ago, and so on until you come to those decisions you expect to make five years in the future. Then go back and briefly describe each decision by using the appropriate symbol as follows:

Your worst decision (W)

Your best decision (B)

A decision you let your parents make for you (P)

A decision you made because others (friends) were doing it, not because you thought it was the best thing to do (F)

A decision where a high risk was involved (R)

A decision you're particularly proud of (PR)

The most important decision you've ever made (MI)

A decision you are facing now which is difficult (D)

A decision you don't look forward to making (DE)

A decision that will have a lot of impact on what you may or may not be able to do five years from now (I)

The most important decision you expect to make in the next three years (FI)

A decision you're looking forward to making (ENJ)

5 YEARS AGO

Decision 1
Decision 2
Decision 3

3 YEARS AGO

Decision 1
Decision 2
Decision 3

1 YEAR AGO

Decision 1
Decision 2
Decision 3

PRESENT

Decision 1
Decision 2
Decision 3

3 YEARS FROM NOW

Decision 1
Decision 2
Decision 3

5 YEARS FROM NOW

Decision 1
Decision 2
Decision 3

EXERCISE 3. It Begins and Ends with You

One of the key requirements for making a good decision is that you have a firm grasp of what you are all about: what you need, what you want today and tomorrow, what strengths and weaknesses you have, and what opportunities you'd like to have in the future. A good way to get an insight into these areas of concern is to do a simple situational analysis. Without paying any attention to the order, fill in the four boxes below with as much specific information as you can. (Don't look back more than three years.) Be as honest as possible. After you've filled in as much information as you can don't be reluctant to ask others, such as your parents and friends, to help you fill in the boxes. Remember, all too often we can put ourselves down (or puff ourselves up) when it isn't necessary or appropriate. Sometimes another view is helpful.

YOUR SITUATIONAL ANALYSIS

What do you have going for you? (strengths)	What are some of your weaknesses?

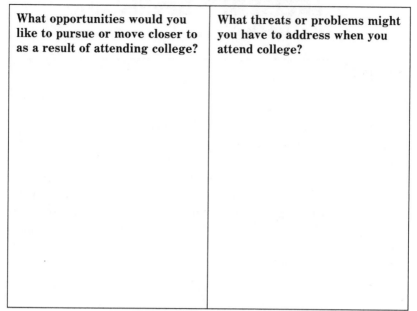

What opportunities would you like to pursue or move closer to as a result of attending college?	What threats or problems might you have to address when you attend college?

Now review the information you've collected. What are some things you have learned about yourself from your situational analysis? Write these observations below and then answer the following questions.

What I learned: _____

_____

_____

_____

_____

What do you think will be easiest for you when you attend college? Why?

_____

_____

_____

_____

_____

Where or with what do you think you'll encounter the most difficulty? Why?

_____

_____

_____

_____

What do you feel is the single greatest opportunity college offers to you? Why?

_____

_____

_____

_____

Are you really ready to take full advantage of a college education? Why?

_____

_____

_____

_____

Don't worry about having a ready answer right away. The important thing is to begin your thought process, because these are the kinds of questions you're going to have to answer if you want to get the most from your college experience. This book is going to ask you to do a lot of thinking about yourself, and before you're done you may have some very different responses to these questions.

EXERCISE 4. Things You Enjoy and Don't Enjoy

Another way to gain insight into your strengths and weaknesses is to make a turn-on and turn-off list. You do this by writing down all the things you enjoy doing in one column and the things you don't enjoy or that flat out turn you off in the second column. As always, be as specific as you can. Your list can include school and nonschool activities, organized or informal, complex or simple. Some examples on the enjoyment side might be basketball, reading, backpacking, skiing, dancing, or being alone. On the dislike side some possibilities could be tests, math, loud music, baby-sitting, or being alone. Go ahead! Complete your own list below.

Things I Enjoy   **Things I Don't Enjoy**

_____   _____

_____   _____

_____   _____

_____   _____

_____   _____

_____   _____

_____   _____

_____   _____

_____   _____

_____   _____

Look at each of the entries and try to figure out why a given item is important, enjoyable, or unenjoyable. Many students find that things in the enjoyable category are things they do well. Although they sometimes don't like to admit it, the turn-offs often reveal a weakness or something they avoid because they feel uncomfortable with it. This is perfectly normal and true, in general, for people of all ages. On the other hand, people who grow and develop throughout their life are those who are willing to address those areas of weakness or discomfort. Many colleges, in fact, will require students to take a wide variety of courses well outside their majors so it becomes impossible to "hide" in your areas of strength or comfort.

This is a long way of saying your college choice will have an element of risk attached to it. In fact, it is possible to take on a high level of risk during the college years by signing up for the most difficult courses, by seeking out professors who really lay on the work, and by pursuing majors that may not lead to automatic employment and a high level of pay upon graduation.

What kind of a risk taker are you? Think about two things you've accomplished over the past two years. Did these accomplishments involve trying something new at the risk of some embarrassment to you? Or did they represent things you were already good at and just repeated at the same level of performance? Or were they things you did because they were so important that you did them without even thinking about the risk that was involved?

Describe one of the biggest risks you've ever taken. _____

_____

_____

_____

_____

_____

_____

What made it worth doing? _____

_____

_____

_____

_____

_____

_____

Would you do it again? Why? _____

_____

_____

_____

_____

_____

_____

CHAPTER

3

Accepting the Challenge— Taking Charge

If the message hasn't been clear it should be: the college choice is yours. Regardless of who makes the decision or whose advice you follow, it is you who will have to live with the consequences of the choice. The more you delay taking charge, the more you will work yourself into what might be called a defensive decision position. You won't have time to research, plan, and implement your choice properly. Most likely, you'll find yourself in a hasty, reactive, panic-stricken situation leading to very disappointing results. Most people who delay their decisions get stuck with the leftovers, and that's as unappetizing as it sounds. There is something to be said for the old truism that the best defense is a good offense. In fact, your best chance to avoid a less than acceptable result in the college choice is to begin to take control. Taking control means to plan, plan, and plan! As you work through your college decision you'll be asked to prepare a number of mini-plans as well as a more elaborate set of plans, which you'll develop once you're accepted.

Before we get to the specifics, let's take a closer look at what the planning process is all about. A good way to view the process is as though you're looking at your life or an aspect of your life through a telescope. The planning process takes you from the broad to the narrow so you're able to focus on some very specific things you want to attain.

To get started, your first plan will be a design for taking charge of the decision itself. That is, you will plan the actions you have to take between March or April of your junior year of high school and March of your senior year to investigate, develop alternatives, make a college choice, and implement that choice after you are accepted. Look at your plan as a vehicle for getting you from where you are now to where you want to be. Keep in mind that your college decision has two components: Which colleges represent the best options for me? Which college will I select once I receive admissions decisions from the colleges to which I've applied?

Since your Take Charge plan is intended to get you to the point where you apply to a number of colleges you think meet your needs and wants, your plan will include all aspects of the decision-making process except the Action and Control stage, which will occur after you hear from the colleges to which you have applied. Let's take a look at our planning telescope to get an idea of what might be included in your Take Charge plan.

COMPONENTS OF YOUR TAKE CHARGE PLAN

Preliminary Stage—Define Decision

Which 6 to 10 colleges will I apply to by January 1?

Decision Stage One—Identification

Step 1.   Determine what my most important values are and why.

Decide which values I want my college choices to accommodate.
Completion date _____

Step 2. Outline specific outcomes that I want or expect from the colleges of my choice.
Completion date _____

Decision Stage Two—Alternative Development

Step 3. List the college options that I know enough about now.

Step 4. Gather additional information about existing alternatives. Develop new alternatives.
Completion date _____

Decision Stage Three—Selection

Step 5. Compare options and determine which are most likely to accommodate my values and priorities.
Completion date _____

Step 6. Fill in information gaps through reading, visits, talking with people.
Completion date _____

Step 7. Select first or most desirable choice and rank remaining colleges in order of preference.
Completion date _____

Decision Stage Four—Action and Control

Step 8. Complete and mail applications.
Completion date _____

Step 9. Make the final enrollment choice.

Step 10. If things don't work out—my contingency plan.

Remember, Steps 9 and 10 will be completed after you hear from your college choices.

As you set up your own Take Charge plan, you can sketch in rough completion dates. When you begin to walk through the actual decision process itself, you'll have a better idea of how much you'll need to do; then you can go back to your plan and fill in firmer dates. To help you estimate, it is a good idea to give yourself at least three months to carry out the steps described above. Some students begin the process of at least general information collecting in their junior year, especially if they are applying for some kind of an early decision. Others find they can do a good job if they start up their Take Charge plan by mid-September of the senior year and stick to the completion dates they have specified from September through December of the senior year. It's probably a good idea to complete the first couple of steps in your plan before you spend a lot of time getting specific college data. In order to know what information will help your decision, you have to determine what is important to you—your priorities and expectations of college.

To get an idea of what your action plan might look like, look at the Sample Take Charge Plan. Keep in mind that, depending on the individual involved, some stages of the plan will take more or less time than shown in the sample.

Thought Starter

Are you ready? If you're ready to decide, you should be able to answer *yes* to these questions.

Are you sure you want to go to college?

Do you accept this choice as your choice?

Are you willing to set up a schedule or plan for this choice?

Define Decision

Which 6 to 10 colleges will I apply to by January 1?

Beginning Date

September 5, Senior Year

Things To Do	**Suggested Time Allotment and Completion Date**
Begin Stage 1. General review of what I know. Collect and examine a major college reference and two or three college catalogs.	Several weeks. By September 30.
Complete Stage 1. Look within, clarify values, identify desirable characteristics, describe outcomes. Select and study information sources.	Two weeks (1 hour a day). By October 31.
Complete Stage 2. Identify 6 to 10 most promising options. Do comparisons and fill in important gaps. Visit colleges if necessary.	One week (1 to 2 hours per day). Campus visit time not included. By November 30.
Complete Stage 3. Make final selections and rank in order of preference. Complete applications. Fine-tune decision.	One week (2 hours per day. By January 1.
Complete Stage 4. Select college for enrollment. Set up plan for monitoring the decision. Think about contingencies or What Ifs. Assess financial aid offers.	As per acceptance received. By May 1.

Building a Solid Foundation for Your Choice

Now that you have completed the important preliminaries, you are ready to begin the decision process. Earlier we defined a decision as something that involves a choice, an action, and a commitment of resources. When looking at the entire decision process, a good way to think about it is to break it into three major actions: looking within, looking around, and looking ahead. The first two steps of the decision process involve looking within, and that is what builds the foundation for all critical and important choices. To the degree that you know what is important to you and why, to the same degree you can make a well-considered decision that you will feel fully committed to. It's worth your while to think about this a bit.

Most people, regardless of where they are in their lives, need to see some kind of worth or payoff in something before they can make an enthusiastic commitment to it. And the more they understand why it is worth doing, the more likely it is they will want to spend their time, energy, or money doing it.

The problem many people have in making decisions is that they have never defined for themselves what is important. So, one day it's one thing and the next it's another. These people have a great deal of difficulty making up their minds because they cannot distinguish between the significant and the insignificant, or the important and the very important. One of the building blocks to making a solid decision is to be able to separate things into the very desirable, the desirable, and the not so desirable alternatives. In short, you need to understand why you are willing to commit to certain things and not to others. You must explore and clarify your values (things you care a lot about) so you are able to understand why you do what you do. This is one of the first steps in being able to come up a winner when you make important decisions.

A good way to begin building an understanding is to take a quick inventory of how you choose to spend your time during a fairly typical week. In Exercise 5, list the things you enjoy doing as well as those you don't necessarily like to do but that represent your choices. Record only the things you feel you can decide to do or not do, not things that others have forced you to do or that the law requires you to do (such as attending school). Then try to estimate the average amount of time you spend on each activity.

As a way to get going, check your calendar, go through your check book, review what you did over the summer or over the last few weekends. You might review how you spent your time during the last week.

EXERCISE 5. My Typical Week

Things I Decide To Do   **Average Time Spent**

_____	_____
_____	_____
_____	_____
_____	_____
_____	_____

Once you have completed your list, examine it carefully and answer the following questions:

- Which activity do you spend most of your time doing? What does that reveal about what is important to you?
- Which activities do you do because you enjoy them? What are some things about these that give you pleasure?
- Which activities do you do for a reason other than enjoyment? What does this tell you about what is important to you?

Were you surprised in any way about how you spend your time? Explain.

_____

_____

_____

_____

Take another close look at your list. What does it tell you about what is important to you? To get you started, pretend that a total stranger was looking at your list. What do you think he or she would learn about you and your priorities? When you identify the things you value, be as specific as possible. For example, if you listen to music a lot, it could mean you are inclined to have an academic interest in music, or you like to be entertained, or perhaps you are learning new ways to express yourself musically; it might indicate you like to get away and have some control over your personal world.

What my list tells me about what is important to me:

_____

_____

_____

_____

_____

_____

_____

_____

_____

_____

_____

Thought Starter

Does the expression "You do what you value" hold true for you? How do you know that?

TIME OUT

You just hit the lottery and you have won $100,000 that you must spend within 30 days. You can divide your purchases, investments, trips, etc., into segments of not less than $10,000 each. How would you spend it??? Write down your answers below.

Purchases/Investment/Other   **Your Reasons**

_____   _____

_____   _____

_____   _____

_____   _____

_____   _____

_____   _____

EXERCISE 6.

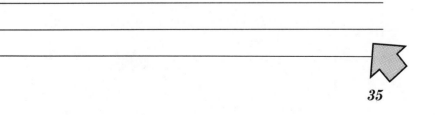

In 25 words or less, explain what your above choices tell about you—your likes, the things you enjoy, and the things you feel are important to you.

_____

_____

_____

_____

_____

Keep in mind this useful definition of values: standards of desirability that enable us to select among alternatives. The next exercise is going to ask you to make some distinctions about what might be important to you in the future. It is a list of things that are important to college-bound students. Using initials, rank each item on the list below in terms of your own priorities as Very Important (VI), Somewhat Important (SI), or Relatively Unimportant (RU). (Remember, the idea here is to put down what you think, *not* what you think others think you should put down as your priorities.)

EXERCISE 7.

_____ Making a lot of money

_____ Becoming an expert in something

_____ Making new friends

_____ Getting a well-paying job upon graduation

_____ Exploring new subjects

_____ Becoming more independent

_____ Getting away from home

_____ Playing on a prestigious team

_____ Learning more about who I am

_____ Gaining self-confidence

_____ Becoming recognized as exceptional in some way

_____ Making a contribution to society

_____ Making contacts for future employment

_____ Living up to the expectations of friends and family

_____ Surpassing the expectations of friends and family

_____ Meeting different people

_____ Becoming more sophisticated and worldly

_____ Learning and gaining knowledge

_____ Being able to be creative and try new things

_____ Encountering a real challenge

_____ Becoming more understanding of others

Use the additional lines below to add any items that are important to you but not listed above.

_____

_____

_____

_____

_____

_____

_____

_____

Not a bad list to have to work with, is it? Because it contains so many things that are at least somewhat important to people, it makes it difficult to separate the most important from the less important. However, that is precisely what critical decision making demands—making distinctions that will enable you to select the best option for yourself. As you begin to try to make these distinctions, you will probably encounter what is called a value conflict—you will have to give up something in order to get something else.

That's precisely what you're going to do now. Look at your list and identify all those items that you have rated very important (VI). Next to each of those items, write down something you have done or committed to in the past year, that proves this item is or has been important to you. For example, if "encounter a real challenge" received one of your top ratings, perhaps the supportive evidence would be that you chose a difficult elective or teacher or undertook a project that had little chance of success. Return to your list and try to come up with the evidence.

What was the result? Was it easy to find examples to support your priority values or did you really have to stretch to find evidence? How many blanks did you come up with? A failure to find something you have done that would indicate a commitment to the priority does not mean it is not important to you. It may mean, however, that there are other things taking up more of your time. If this is true, you should ask yourself why.

The following exercise will make you take a closer look at what you really value. We call it a value clarification exercise. As you begin to evaluate colleges and what they offer you, this clarification effort will pay off; you'll know what your priorities are in choosing a college.

Now return to your list one more time. This time identify the five most important statements on the list for you. Then, rank them from one to five. Your absolutely top choice should be number one.

YOUR FIVE TOP VALUES

1. _____

2. _____

3. _____

4. _____

5. _____

Look at your five items. What do they say about you? In less than 100 words, pretend you are trying to market yourself to a college. Convince the college you should be accepted based upon your top priority value statements. Don't groan! This isn't a waste of time! It will be good practice for completing the essay portion of some of your college applications (see Step 8).

EXERCISE 8. Marketing Your Value Profile

Why You Should Accept Me Based Upon My Five Top Value Statements

_____

_____

_____

_____

_____

_____

_____

_____

_____

_____

Give your essay to somebody to read. Does it make sense to them? Can they identify what is important to you from the contents of your letter? Do they agree that those are the values you have _demonstrated_ in the past as having importance to you? Good people to share with are parents, a friend who will "tell it like it is," a teacher, or some other adult who has worked with you closely over the past one or two years.

By working through the last exercises, you have probably collected enough information to give you a good start on Step 1 of the decision process. Let's take time to summarize what you have learned. Write down the following pieces of information about yourself:

These things are important to me _____

_____

_____

_____

_____

This is why they are important _____

_____

_____

_____

_____

Some things I've done to support my commitment to these values

_____

_____

_____

_____

_____

Since you are going to rely on an accurate sense of your values throughout the college choice process, it is very important that you understand that at the bottom of everything you do, every decision you make, there lies a value judgment of some sort. It comes down to this—people will not do things, they will not commit resources, and they will not be turned on to anything unless it has some perceived value payoff. For example, we know smoking is harmful, but even some doctors continue to smoke. Why? Because in some way the smoker has made a value judgment which may say, "The *possibility* of a healthier life is not worth it if I have to give up the pleasure I get from smoking."

Note the value conflict—in this case, health versus pleasure. For another person it might mean health versus the prospect of gaining weight (or appearance). Think about your own situation. You may give up pleasure to study. Why? You go out for a team requiring several hours of practice each day when you could be with your boyfriend or girlfriend instead. Why?

All people differ somewhat when it comes to what is important to them. We learn about what is important from many different sources: parents, society, school, friends, religious teachings, personal experiences, and so on. Because we learn from different sources and at different times in our lives, the things important to us may change over time. Think about your own situation. Here you are, thinking about college. You've completed most of your formal education (11 or 12 years), and you're about to make an important decision about the future that will in some way have an impact on the rest of your life. Given this situation, what are some things important to you now that were not so important when you were in eighth or ninth grade? Jot these down. What are some other things you expect to be important, say, four or five years from now? Jot these down. See the point? Your values have changed, and these changes will have an impact on your decisions at various points in your life.

Things important to me now

_____

_____

_____

_____

_____

Things I expect to be important _____ years from now

_____

_____

●

Finally, because the importance of things changes over time and even from decision to decision, you may find yourself reordering your top priorities from time to time to make the most appropriate decision at that moment. For example, you may have many friends at this time of your life, so making new ones is not a big priority for you because you've pretty much accommodated that value. Now, suppose you go away to a school where you know absolutely nobody. And suppose you are facing a difficult exam in a day or two but a group of people in your dorm want you to go with them to a big get-acquainted party at one of the fraternities on campus. You know you need the study time to get the grade you want. On the other hand, making new friends is also a top priority, and this party seems to be a good way to address it. What will you do? What value will drive your decision—friends or good grades?

To continue the process of sorting out and clarifying your own significant values, try to work through some of the dilemmas below. Decide what you would do and why. Then identify which values (standards of desirability) you have applied. Take the time to write down your answers. You might find it useful to refer back to your list of value statements.

Situation 1

You have read about the selectivity of various colleges of interest to you and have found that the academic competition at these schools is very keen. You have always been in the top 10 percent of your high school class, with mostly A grades in your courses. Students at these colleges seem just like you, and it occurs to you that all students will not make the top 10 percent with the kind of competition that will be faced at that college. Friends you've talked with, with grades similar to yours, have had a difficult time getting B's in similar colleges. If you do get accepted, will you go even though schools with lesser academic standards would likely make your being in the top 10 percent a pretty sure thing?

_____

_____

What would you decide? What values drove your decision? Why are these values the most important priorities for you?

_____

_____

_____

Situation 2

You have been accepted to two schools. One is a small college, not very well known but with a fine reputation. The other acceptance is from one of the most prestigious colleges in the country. When you tell others about it, they all assume you are going to attend the most prestigious school. Even more obvious is the pride your parents exhibit when they tell their friends that you were accepted by this school. You have visited all of the schools, and it is clear to you the less well known school is your best choice. The pressure is getting to you, and you want to please your parents. What would you decide? Why?

_____

_____

What values drove your decision? _____

_____

_____

Situation 3

You're not a very good writer and you are having a difficult time doing the essay on your college application, which you know is an important part of the application at that college. You know you are supposed to do this writing by yourself. Your parents have offered to write it up for you, and you know other kids who get it done this way. What would you do? Why?

_____

What does this decision say about what is important to you?

_____

_____

Situation 4

You are applying for a job that you want very much. On the application there is a question asking whether or not you have ever used drugs. Once or twice you have, in fact, smoked marijuana. You have also had beer and other alcoholic drinks at parties you have attended over the past year. The question is more than a yes or no response; you can offer an explanation. What do you do? Why?

_____

_____

What values were important in this situation? _____

_____

_____

Situation 5

You very much want to play intercollegiate athletics. One of the colleges you're considering has an excellent program, but the people who make the team are usually on some kind of an athletic scholarship. The chances of making the team as a walk-on are very slim; yet if you do make it, you'll be playing at a very high level of competition and getting a lot of exposure via TV and the news media. What do you do? Why?

_____

_____

In this situation, what values might be in conflict? _____

_____

_____

Situation 6

The school of your dreams has accepted you. It's the place you have always wanted to go. There is one major hitch. You are in need of financial assistance. The college does not offer you enough in grants, loans, and scholarships to cover your expenses. If you go to this school, you will have to work many hours a week in order to pay your bills. It may even be necessary to take off a year and work in order to have enough money. Another school, with a good reputation, has offered you what amounts to an all-expenses-covered financial package. You hate to give up your dream, but you wonder if the extra work will jeopardize your success. What would you decide? Why?

_____

_____

What values drove your decision? _____

_____

Situation 7

You are in the running for top academic honors. It means a lot because the top student from each school in your state gets a full scholarship to the state university. During an end-of-year science test, you see your main competitor for high honors taking answers from another student's paper during the test. There is no doubt in your mind cheating is going on. What do you decide? Why?

_____

_____

What values would you be considering in this situation?

_____

_____

The Forces That
Drive Your Decisions

As you continue working toward making your college choice, you'll encounter similar value dilemmas. Indeed, throughout your life you will have to make many decisions where there won't be a clear, obvious way to go. This is when you'll need to take an even closer look at what you value. As you try to sort things out, there are two major pitfalls to avoid.

The first is what I call the historical agenda—those things you've heard so often they become an automatic part of your decision making. Some of these include: smart kids should go to college after high school; work hard and you'll be rewarded; listen to your elders; honesty is the best policy. You've heard most of them, and it *is* important to pay attention to these historical "truths."

Nevertheless, in a given situation you may find the historical truth is not the best way to go. For example, honesty is *not* always the best policy. To illustrate, let's say your very best friend Tom is not very attractive. In fact, he may be downright ugly. You also know Tom is very concerned about his looks. One day when you're together, Tom asks you about his looks. In this case would honesty be the best policy? Got the point? As you can see, the college choice, or any other choice, should not be automatically governed by things we have learned from history. Consider what you have learned, yes! But look at the situation carefully. Things that may have worked in the past may not apply to today's or tomorrow's decisions. It may be a totally different ball game.

The second pitfall is even more serious. This is what might be called the Ought To value agenda. It is what most people around you, including parents, friends, teachers, and others, think you ought to do. You can feel the pressure to go along with the crowd, to do the obvious, or to do what other people think you should do. It is a difficult situation because those who are giving Ought To advice are well meaning. They want the best for you. You will be better prepared to face this pressure if you've studied the decision process in this book.

Remember, regardless of what advice you get or who gives it, *you*, not that person, have to live with the consequences of accepting that advice. Keep in mind that every person is unique. A decision, even if it is obvious to others, may not match your special needs and dreams. Given the rapid change taking place in all areas of living, Ought To concepts rarely keep pace, nor do they represent especially creative thinking.

It is difficult to go against the Ought To agendas, to go in a direction opposite or removed from what others think you should do. Of course, if what others think you should do corresponds with your top value, then the Ought To agenda may be a good course for you. On the other hand, if you're interested in pursuing what is uniquely important to you, you might have to reject the Ought To course of action. Being fully

Thought Starter

Here are some common Ought Tos you may have to face when you make your college choice. Add some you've been hearing from other people.

- If you do major in something like art, be sure to minor in something practical like computer programming.
- You should go to a place where you know a lot of people.
- If you're paying a lot for college, the contacts you make ought to help you later in life.

Add your own: _____

_____

_____

aware of both what is important to you and why it is important is the best guarantee that you will feel confident about your choice when it differs from what others expect or when you have to stand up for things that are special to you.

Now that you have taken your first detailed look at yourself and your priorities, let's move on to the next step in our decision process.

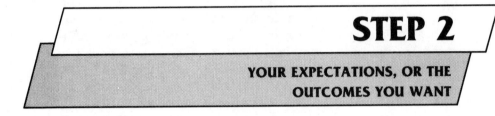

STEP 2

YOUR EXPECTATIONS, OR THE OUTCOMES YOU WANT

What payoffs or returns do you want to get from the college experience—from the college of your choice? In Step 2, you will begin to answer this question. You will learn to identify your expectations, or the outcomes you want from your college choice. Sounds simple. Unfortunately, too often we make decisions without first having a clear sense of what we want to accomplish. If you were to make a decision based upon only a vague idea of what you want and a small amount of consideration, you are apt to get less than you could have had if you had done some planning and thinking. A second danger evolves as well. If you don't think about good and bad outcomes before you make a decision, there's a good chance you'll be unprepared for what does occur.

Decision Disaster. Why?

Bill had heard about the university of his choice for many years. After all, his father had attended and so had his sister. Bill had heard about the wonderful experiences both had had, and he had attended a variety of events at the university. His choice was easy. He was expected to follow the family tradition and he did. Bill found the university to be a nice place but not for him. He hadn't realized how different a student population of 10,000 would be, especially compared with the small high school he'd attended where he knew everybody and they knew him.

As you can see, Bill fell into a common decision trap. He assumed he would find the same kind of outcomes in a college that people he loved and admired had. Bill forgot to think about his own needs and values.

The skilled decision maker takes a good look at expectations and desired outcomes. By getting a handle on what you want to achieve, you'll know what information to collect, have a better idea of how to go about achieving it, and have a clearer understanding of why it's worth achieving. Consequently, this is a critical part of your choice process. It can be viewed as your first attempt to use some of the things you know about yourself (your values) to get some of the things you want (future results). This first effort to look ahead will be pretty general. You'll get more and more specific as you complete future decision steps. Although the focus may be general, it should not be and cannot be sloppy! So you'll need to do some good, clear thinking about what you want from your college experience.

Some Typical Expectations About College

The following statements are from students who were asked to describe some expectations they had regarding college.

I want to get a good education.
I expect to be trained so I can get a job.
College should help me make a lot of money.
I want a college education to help me learn more about myself.
I want to learn something new.
College should enable me to meet different people.
I want to have the opportunity to write for a real newspaper.

49

While these expectations or objectives are OK for getting you to begin to think about the future, most are too vague to provide a real focus. For example, what is a "good" education? How much is "a lot" of money? To what extent will training get one a good job? And, couldn't we all learn something new without going to college? Before you begin writing your own general objectives, study the following guidelines for clear and useful writing. Your statements about what you expect to achieve or attain as a result of going to college should be:

Specific

Reduce the details to something that others would be able to understand immediately.

I expect a college education to give me at least one marketable skill that would enable me to get a job within three months of graduation.

Measurable

Goals or results that cannot be measured or at least described in detail tend to be less than helpful because you will have no way of knowing when you've attained what you want.

I expect to start my first job out of college with a salary of not less than $25,000.

I will join the varsity basketball team for three years.

I will travel to and live in at least two foreign countries for at least three months each before my senior year.

Attainable

Any objective you strive for should be attainable. Once you recognize something is not attainable, you become turned off and frustrated.

I expect to make the staff of the college paper. (This seems reasonable based upon my high school experience and what I've learned about what you have to do to make the staff of the college paper.)

Relevant

This brings us back to our values. Normally you will not make the effort required to reach for something if you don't perceive a payoff that is of value to you. For example, it may sound nice to say you want to meet different people, but are you willing to reach out, to go beyond an accidental meeting that might lead to a relationship? Is the result (a relationship) worth the effort (reaching out) to you, or in other words, is it of value to you?

Time Referenced

It is helpful to attach some kind of time frame or schedule to your question for certain results. A schedule keeps you honest about whether or not you're serious in your pursuit, and it also provides you with a way to measure your progress.

By the end of my junior year, I will have become fluent in one foreign language.

By the end of my senior year I will have had at least four different summer job experiences.

Defined

You need to understand what you are after, and that will require definition and more definition. For example, if you are shooting for making a lot of money fast, you'll have to define those terms ("a lot" and "fast") so you know exactly what you're after. Two examples of well-defined goals are:

I expect to be earning $50,000 per year in today's dollars by the time I reach age 30.

By age 35, regardless of location, I expect to own a house, a new car, and have $25,000 in my savings account.

To this point, you've covered a lot of material that will be instrumental in taking your next decision steps. To make sure you don't lose sight of the good thinking you've done, review and complete the learning summary and update on the following pages.

Using the above guidelines as models, try to describe at least five outcomes you expect from your college experience. Make sure they are specific, measurable, and attainable over a defined period of time. Is the payoff really important to you?

Five things I expect to attain from my college experience:

_____

_____

_____

_____

_____

You'll have several chances to expand upon and clarify these statements later. At the moment, keep them as a ready reference, which you'll need as you move closer to determining your college preferences.

Learning Summary and Update

1. What factor do you think will have the greatest influence on your college choice?

_____

_____

_____

_____

2. What's your number one reason for attending college? Why?

_____

_____

_____

3. What are the four stages of the critical decision process?

_____

_____

_____

4. What do the things you don't enjoy doing tell you about yourself?

_____

_____

_____

5. What are two things you need to do in Stage 2 of your college decision?

_____

_____

_____

6. Where and how do you spend most of your time during the week? Why?

_____

_____

_____

_____

7. What were the five things you identified as being most important to you in the future?

_____

_____

_____

_____

8. What values did you discover in the seven situations you were asked to resolve? List them.

_____

_____

_____

_____

9. Give an example of a good measurable outcome or expectation of the college experience.

_____

_____

_____

_____

10. How would you define a "successful" college experience for you? Keep your definition to less than 25 words.

_____

_____

_____

_____

Congratulations! If you have completed this book to this point, you have done more thinking about the college decision than most students ever do!

Looking Around: Getting Beyond the Obvious

Up to now, you've been looking within; you've turned your information search inward, and using what you know, and perhaps what you didn't know you knew, you have begun to draw some conclusions about the results or outcomes you expect from the college experience. Now it's time to begin looking around and doing it creatively. The looking-around activities include identifying some promising college options and filling in any remaining information gaps to enable you to identify 6 to 10 options that seem to best meet your needs and expectations.

There is a wealth of excellent information available describing thousands of colleges. However, if you tried to read one of these directories or guidebooks without first knowing what you were looking for, you'd end up confused and overwhelmed by information. In addition, you'd probably be no closer to a decision than when you started, and you would have wasted a lot of valuable time.

Separating the Desirable from
the Less Desirable

So before actually identifying options and gathering additional information, you need to do some preparation. Preparation in this case means determining the specific college characteristics you want. Your specifications will enable you to make distinctions between the many options you have available to you and to accept or reject alternatives in a well-considered and timely fashion. Since you are the decider and you are unique, your list may differ from your friends' and from your parents'. That's OK and to be expected. It is important to develop your own specifications first before you share your list with others. Later, add those ideas you have omitted from your first attempts. Caution! Don't add a specification unless you are clear about why you think you should add it.

A good way to go about compiling your list of desired characteristics is to imagine you are interviewing a large number of colleges to find the one that is most suitable for you. In making up your list, you are really developing a set of interview questions that will enable you to accept or reject any number of these "applicants" for your acceptance. There are three categories into which you can group your interview questions. The first category, and probably the one with the most questions, can be called the Right Fit category. In this category, you're going to explore all those aspects of a potential college that will match the kinds of things you've learned about yourself: your strengths and weaknesses and the opportunities you wish to explore in college. Some questions might be: Does it have a strong mathematics department? Does it have an intercollegiate baseball program? Is it within 300 miles of my home? Does it have fewer than 5,000 students?

The second category of specifications is called Freedom to Act and Decide. This category of specifications focuses on the amount of choice, flexibility, independence, and freedom you will have at a given college when it comes to choosing a major, travel-abroad opportunities, required courses, policies about dropping out for a year and working, and being able to select a roommate or a living facility such as off-campus housing.

The final category is Standards of Performance. In this category you'll look at the quality of the institution, what its graduates do upon graduation, the rate of admission to top-flight graduate schools, the companies that come to the college to recruit students for jobs, the levels of academic or athletic competitiveness, and the reputation of the faculty.

By grouping your specifications into these categories, you'll be able to keep your focus during your "interviews." As you go along you may find some questions need to be dropped and others added to enhance the effectiveness of the interview. In the space provided below, try to identify at least five specifications for each category. Examples are provided to help you get started.

EXERCISE 9. Which Colleges Meet My Specs?

Right Fit
Example: Does this college have coed dorms?

1. _____

2. _____

3. _____

4. _____

5. _____

Freedom to Act and Decide
Example: Is it possible to take a pass-fail instead of a letter grade?

1. _____

2. _____

3. _____

4. _____

5. _____

Standards of Performance

Example: What percentage of classes are taught by graduate assistants as opposed to full-time faculty?

1. _____

2. _____

3. _____

4. _____

5. _____

Review your list of questions. Have you forgotten anything? Using the items below as idea stimulators, add any additional specifications that you think are important to you: social climate, diversity of the student body, student body size, financial aid availability, cost of tuition, on-campus housing availability, cars permitted, parking, tutoring program, exchange programs with other schools, male–female ratio, most important admissions requirement, weather, availability of transportation to major cities, number of students who transfer out after one year, job possibilities in the local community.

Additions

_____

_____

_____

_____

_____

Determining Your Gotta Haves

Listing specifications is a useful exercise to get you thinking, but it's not specific enough to help you begin to reduce hundreds of possibilities to a dozen or so "best" prospects. A good technique for sharpening your focus is the Gotta Have and Like to Have elimination exercise. It goes something like this. Think about all of the characteristics you like or don't like, and then make a list of those things that must be part of any college you choose. Your Musts or Gotta Haves represent your very basic requirements, your very top priorities. On the flip side, think of them as your Eliminators, for when they're not present you cannot accept that college option.

In putting together your Gotta Haves, remember the rules for writing clear characteristics. State things that are specific and measurable, such as: "A college must have off-campus housing, intercollegiate basketball, an economics major, and a student population of not more than 2,000." Forcing yourself to measure specific things will push you to define what you want more clearly. Even if things are difficult to measure, such as school spirit, superior faculty, or a diversity of students, you can push your definition so you are at least describing in clear terms what these things mean to you. For example, school spirit might be measured by the percentage of students who attend home football games or by the number of students who remain at the college for the full four years. Likewise, your definition of a superior faculty might be that teachers give considerable time to students outside the classroom. In all cases, the measure you use is *your* measure or description; it reflects what *you* feel is important or basic in terms of meeting your requirements. Developing your Gotta Haves requires much thought.

Make a quick personal assessment: What are three Gotta Haves you would include in buying a new car?

_____

_____

_____

EXERCISE 10. Gotta Haves and Like to Haves

In the space below, write down four to eight of your Gotta Haves. Remember, the more you have, the more Eliminators you have. If you have very few basic requirements, you won't eliminate very many colleges and you'll still have a large field of options to choose from.

Gotta Haves: My basic requirements. The college *must* have these if I am to apply.

_____

_____

_____

_____

_____

_____

_____

_____

Write down your Like to Haves below, and then go back and grade each with an A, B, or C to indicate Very Special, Special, or Somewhat Special. You can have as many of each grade on your list as you wish.

Like to Haves: Things that are important to me but not absolutely necessary.

_____

_____

_____

_____

_____

_____

_____

_____

_____

If you're having trouble identifying your Gotta and Like to Haves (and even if you're not), try this quick warm-up exercise. Suppose you have been asked by your college to identify those characteristics you want in a roommate. List them in the space below, differentiating between the Must Haves and Like to Haves.

Three traits a roommate *must* have:

1. _____

2. _____

3. _____

An additional five traits I'd *like* my roommate to have:

1. _____

2. _____

3. _____

4. _____

5. _____

There's one additional step you should do to sharpen your thinking about your Musts. Before you actually make a commitment to your list of Musts, think about all the things the colleges of your choice must *not* have. Make a list of these below, and then write down why.

**Things the College Must
Not Have** **Why????????**

_____ _____

_____ _____

_____ _____

_____ _____

_____ _____

You will continue to fine-tune and make use of your Gotta, Like to, and Must Not Haves as you progress through this book. Before moving on, take time to answer the following Thought Starter questions.

Thought Starter

Return to your lists of characteristics and identify your basic requirements and any other of the important considerations you have. As you do this, ask yourself:

Does this make sense in terms of what I said is important to me? Why?

_____

Does it support the results I have specified relating to my college experience? How?

_____

Will these characteristics move me closer to those things I've identified as being important to me five years from now? Explain.

_____

_____

1. Consult a college directory such as *The College Handbook*. Compare your list of characteristics to three college profiles: small college (2,000 or fewer students), medium (5,000 to 8,000 students), large (10,000 or more students). What characteristics are missing from your list? Add them to your lists below:

Gotta Haves added:

_____

_____

_____

Like to Haves added:

_____

_____

_____

_____

2. Identify the three outcomes that you think are most important for you to realize from your college education. Be sure they are specific and measurable, and that they accommodate those things about the future you rate as very important to you.

1. _____

2. _____

3. _____

3. Review a college catalog. Identify all the programs that offer some kind of financial assistance to students.

Looking Around: Getting Creative

An alternative that is out of sight may as well not exist. As with most critical decisions, many options exist that you are apt to miss for one reason or another. You may, as do many students, go with the obvious; you may quit looking around too soon because it is too time-consuming; you may have an inaccurate opinion of yourself so you underestimate your possibilities.

This chapter is designed to keep you from closing the door on what might be your best opportunities. That's why this part of the decision process is one of the most critical: it's the time you begin to reach beyond familiar things and come up with new ideas that will influence what you may or may not be able to do in the future.

In this chapter you'll complete Steps 3 and 4 of your critical decision process: identifying alternatives you know about (Step 3) and expanding them through creative thinking techniques that will push you beyond the easy and obvious to the more unusual choices (Step 4). Work through these steps carefully and thoughtfully, taking a confident step from where you are now to where you want to be in the future. Get ready to do some creative thinking!

STEP 3

Your first task is very straightforward, and it will serve as your base or push-off point for generating new ideas. List below the college options you know something about already, then write down several characteristics for each school.

Colleges I Know About   **What I Know About Them**

Now make a second list of schools you've heard about that sound interesting but that you know very little about. Write down what you know about each school.

Some Interesting Options   **What I Know About Them**

_____   _____

                              _____

                              _____

_____   _____

                              _____

                              _____

_____   _____

                              _____

                              _____

These two tasks have focused on things you know about already. Try to step into the future for a moment. Given what you have learned about yourself and your priorities, and considering the characteristics you have developed in the previous chapter, imagine what your *ideal* college would be like. Paint a picture of this ideal covering the following features. Add your own features to make the ideal college as vivid as possible.

EXERCISE 11. My Ideal College

What it would look like: _____

_____

_____

What most of the students would be like: _____

_____

_____

_____

What kind of academic success I would have: _____

_____

_____

_____

What the school spirit would be: _____

_____

_____

_____

The kind of relationships students would have with faculty:

_____

_____

_____

_____

What impact the college would have on how I feel about myself:

_____

_____

_____

_____

_____

How the college would address my strengths and weaknesses:

_____

_____

_____

_____

_____

What I'd be able to do upon graduation from this college:

_____

_____

_____

_____

Other features: _____

_____

_____

_____

_____

Now go back to your three lists of colleges. What information needs do you have for each? Write them below.

Colleges I Know About

_____

_____

_____

_____

Some Interesting Options

_____

_____

_____

_____

My Ideal College

_____

_____

_____

_____

_____

Now you have some idea of what your information needs are, but where do you go to find the answers? There are five information resources you have at your disposal as you begin to refine your decisions.

Things to Read   College directories, individual college catalogs, articles about applying to college, and so forth.

People to Talk To	Teachers, friends, guidance counselors, parents, college officials, college students.
Places to Visit	Admissions offices, college fairs, college campuses, financial aid offices.
Things to Experience	College-level courses, living away from home, working with college students, independent study options.
Self-Knowledge	Your talents, special skills, unusual accomplishments, commitment to others, things that really bug you.

The information-gathering phase of your decision takes a fair amount of time. It is the beginning of your efforts to fill in your information gaps so you can distinguish clearly among your possible choices. The process begins with the inventory of what you know and then turns to what you don't know. You should begin to fill in these information gaps from the latter part of your junior year to about November of your senior year.

Decision Disaster. Why?

Eric was always impressed by status items—cars, clothes, and so forth. When it came to college, Eric's decision was swayed by so-called status or "in" schools. After getting accepted, it was clear to Eric that he didn't care for the students he had met on a campus visit, and he had some real doubts as to the quality of the fine arts program, which was his early choice for a major.

Take a moment and draw up an action plan for the information-gathering part of your decision process. List in Exercise 12 the information resources and the things you anticipate doing for each. Tie each action to a completion date. For example, you might want to call or write in for various college catalogs by a given date and then review and summarize by a later date.

EXERCISE 12. Identifying and Using More Resources

	Action	Begin/ Complete
Things to Read		
		/
		/
		/
		/
		/
		/
People to Talk To		
		/
		/
		/
		/
		/
		/
Places to Visit		
		/
		/
		/
		/
		/

Don't forget to add experiences that may help you with your information search, as well as self-study. Of course if you did review the first few chapters of this book you have taken some important steps toward understanding your priorities and expectations.

As you continue your search for the best college option, don't get bogged down in lazy or obvious thinking. Try for something new or different! Here are some things to observe if you want to be your creative best.

Look for more than what you have in mind already. It's a bad practice to identify options (usually the obvious ones) and to focus only on those options. In the process, you prevent yourself from finding what may be the best choice for you.

Play out the possible before you consider what's impossible. The human mind is quite capable of being too hard on itself. Virtually anything is possible as long as you don't see it as impossible. So before you eliminate any of your options, ask yourself, "What is possible about this alternative?"

Practice constructive discontent. If a choice seems very obvious or if it seems to evolve without a great deal of thinking on your part, it may be too easy—a sign you haven't given the decision enough thought. Force yourself to look at the negatives. What could go wrong with your choice?

Escape from bad habits. Getting in a comfortable groove may become a bad rut. If you're like most people, you probably enjoy those things you do well. That's just fine, but you may want to break out of those comfort zones. Why? Because you will learn more about yourself and probably profit from taking a few risks. In addition, things you find easy to do may not represent the long-term turn-on you'll get from meeting the challenge of doing something different, new, and more difficult.

Now apply creative thinking to your college options. In addition to those schools you've identified, find one new alternative by doing the following:

- Investigate a college you have never heard about before.
- Consider a school you think is an impossibility for you. Investigate all aspects of that school before you give up on it.
- Study the option you think is one of your most promising. Find at least five negatives about it.
- Locate a college environment in which you'd feel uncomfortable because you'd be forced to address or deal with some of your weaknesses—some of the things you don't do really well.

How do you locate fresh alternatives? By visiting one or more of the information resources described on pages 70–71. A good way to begin your search is to frame a question you want that particular resource to answer. The following examples may help:

Resource: Guidance Counselor (People to Talk To).

Question: How do I find out about some new college options—ones I don't know about?

Resource: College Directory or Guidebook (Things to Read).

Question: How do I find out about the financial aid programs of schools that seem too expensive for me?

Resource: Campus Trip (Places to Visit).

Question: What are five things students don't like about this place?

Resource: Taking a New Course (Things to Experience).

Question: What are the payoffs for doing something that is not easy for me to do well?

Having tapped these additional resources, you can now add the new and promising alternatives you have identified. These represent your first attempt to be creative and to go beyond what everybody expects you to be doing. Remember, at this stage of your decision you're merely exploring possibilities; you have not made a commitment to anything. Since you have covered a lot of territory thus far, take a brief time out and summarize your progress on Decision Step 3.

TIME OUT

ALTERNATIVES YOU KNOW A LOT ABOUT

_____

_____

_____

_____

Information Gaps

_____

_____

_____

_____

Resources to Pursue

_____

_____

_____

ALTERNATIVES YOU KNOW A LITTLE ABOUT

_____

_____

_____

_____

Information Gaps

_____

_____

_____

_____

Resources to Pursue

_____

_____

_____

_____

Revisit your "ideal" college descriptions.
Which alternatives seem to meet those ideals?

_____

_____

_____

_____

_____

_____

_____

_____

**What new alternatives do you want to pursue
now that you've identified them?**

_____

_____

_____

_____

_____

_____

_____

_____

_____

_____

STEP 4

**IDENTIFYING
NEW ALTERNATIVES**

You've already begun your move from Step 3 to Step 4. Now you're going to get much more specific. Your next task is to do some hard and clever detective work. To wit, you'll be applying your list of desired characteristics (your Gotta Haves and Like to Haves) to the options you've identified to date. Not only will this help you see additional information needs, but it will also begin to highlight some major differences between the options.

EXERCISE 13. Rating Your College Options

List your most promising college options along the top of the chart. Along the side, list the features that you've Gotta Have, the ones you'd Like to Have, and those you Do Not Want (refer back to your lists on pages 60–62). Then fill in the grid, using checks to mean the college has the feature you want or would like to have, and "No!" if it has features you do not want. Use question marks if you need more information.

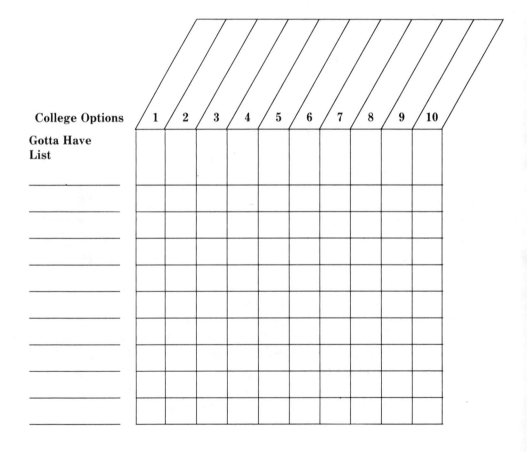

College Options | 1 / 2 / 3 / 4 / 5 / 6 / 7 / 8 / 9 / 10

Gotta Have List

College Options

	1	2	3	4	5	6	7	8	9	10
Like to Have List										
_____										
_____										
_____										
_____										
_____										
_____										
_____										
_____										
_____										

Do Not Want List										
_____										
_____										
_____										
_____										
_____										
_____										
_____										
_____										
_____										

You're not done yet. Put on your detective hat and apply your characteristics to the five new or creative alternatives you identified earlier.

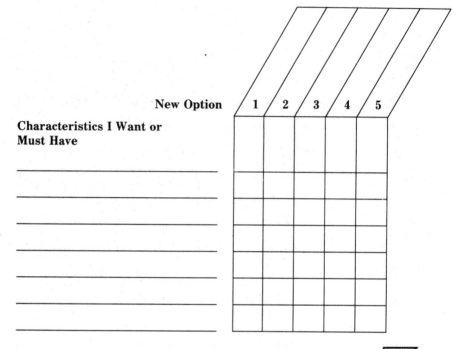

New Option 1 2 3 4 5

Characteristics I Want or Must Have

Which colleges seem to be most promising based upon how well they met your list of desirable or undesirable characteristics? See if you can place them in one of the four categories listed in Exercise 14.

Decision Disaster. Why?

Ralph waited until the last minute to make his decision about college. Then he fired off a dozen applications just to play it safe. He was accepted by eight schools. At this point, he can't decide so he's decided to let his parents tell him what they think would be the best choice. He plans to get his counselor's advice as well.

EXERCISE 14. Putting It Together: The Best and the Worst

Most Promising Options

_____

_____

_____

_____

_____

_____

_____

Not Promising

_____

_____

_____

_____

_____

_____

Somewhat Promising Alternatives

_____

_____

_____

_____

_____

_____

May Be Promising but I Don't Know Enough about These

_____

_____

_____

_____

_____

_____

Steps 3 and 4 point out the information gaps in your decision thus far. The next chapter will give you some specific techniques for filling in those gaps. Before you move on, review and complete the learning update.

Learning Summary and Update

A. List the three most important outcomes you expect from your college experience.

    1. _____

    2. _____

    3. _____

B. Describe at least three things you need to know more about before you can make a decision about college.

    1. _____

    2. _____

    3. _____

C. Identify information sources that would help you fill in the information gaps you've spotted in B.

This Info Resource   **Would Help Fill This Info Gap**

_____   _____

_____   _____

_____   _____

_____   _____

You've begun to separate your most promising options from the less promising by using your information skills and by closing a number of your information gaps. Remember: If a college does not meet one or more of your Musts, it is a good bet for elimination. Before you do take it off your list, make sure your Must *is* a basic necessity.

Using
Information
As Power

Information is power. Use this power to overcome the gaps or uncertainties you have come up against in your research. In this chapter you'll take two additional steps to reduce the uncertainty of your choice—Step 5: Comparing Your Alternatives and Their Outcomes; and Step 6: Describing the Information You Need to Move Ahead. Graphically, these two steps would look like this:

COLLEGE A

Possible Outcomes	Information Needed
70% to grad school Technical studies Make baseball team	Quality of grad schools Chances of walk-on to make varsity

COLLEGE B

Possible Outcomes	Information Needed
60% to grad school Everyone makes team Tech studies at another location	Quality of off-campus tech studies Level of varsity competition

COLLEGE C

Possible Outcomes	Information Needed
40% to grad school Small chance of making team Known for tech faculty	What non-grad schoolers do Non-varsity opportunities Faculty-student relationships

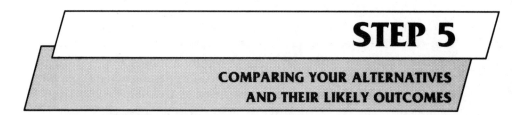

STEP 5

COMPARING YOUR ALTERNATIVES AND THEIR LIKELY OUTCOMES

The student in the above sample is obviously interested in knowing about the percentage of students from each school that go on to graduate school, the availability and quality of technical studies, and the chances of playing varsity baseball. Which possible outcomes are you most interested in knowing about?

In Exercise 15, complete your own Alternative/Outcomes Comparison chart for six of your most promising college options. You can add more options if you wish. Be sure to put down any information you know is a fact. Anything you can't rate as factual goes in the Information Needs column.

EXERCISE 15. Alternatives/ Outcomes Comparison Chart

Alternatives	Outcomes I Know About	Information Needs/Gaps
_____	_____	_____
	_____	_____
	_____	_____
_____	_____	_____
	_____	_____
	_____	_____
_____	_____	_____
	_____	_____
	_____	_____
_____	_____	_____
	_____	_____
	_____	_____
_____	_____	_____
	_____	_____
	_____	_____
_____	_____	_____
	_____	_____
	_____	_____

As you gather information, you'll see that your choices will become much, much clearer, enabling you to distinguish between the positives and negatives of each. Your information search and analysis will move you through the unknown to a real sense of the probabilities relating to your possible outcomes.

1. Unknown Outcomes

2. Uncertain Outcomes

3. Knowing the Chances of an Outcome Happening

4. Knowing Something Will Happen for Sure

The point you're most concerned about reaching is point 3, where you'll have a very good idea about the chance or likelihood of the outcome you want occurring. In most cases, you will not reach point 4 because very few things are for sure. Decision outcomes occur in the future; and in order to be certain that you will get what you want, you'd have to be able to predict the future with absolute accuracy!

A well-made decision will give you the best chance of getting the results you want. In addition, because you are thinking things through in advance, you will be better prepared if something you don't like does occur.

From this point on, all the information you evaluate will be put in two categories: what speaks for and what speaks against your college options. This is called your Information Power Chart. It will be very helpful as you begin to choose one option over another.

Thought Starter

Try to think of a decision you've made or expect to make in the near future. Can you give an example of a decision you made in which you knew for sure what was going to happen?

INFORMATION POWER CHART

COLLEGE

FOR	AGAINST
Outcomes likely	
Values	
Characteristics	

COLLEGE

FOR	AGAINST
Outcomes Likely	
Values	
Characteristics	

INFORMATION POWER CHART

COLLEGE

FOR	AGAINST
Outcomes Likely	
Values	
Characteristics	

COLLEGE

FOR	AGAINST
Outcomes Likely	
Values	
Characteristics	

INFORMATION POWER CHART

COLLEGE

FOR	AGAINST
Outcomes Likely	
Values	
Characteristics	

COLLEGE

FOR	AGAINST
Outcomes Likely	
Values	
Characteristics	

Review your Information Power Chart. What options are still in the running? Were you able to eliminate any colleges? What differences have begun to emerge among your possibilities? What are some of these differences?

College Options	Distinctions of This Option
_____	_____
	_____
_____	_____
	_____
_____	_____
	_____
_____	_____
	_____
_____	_____
	_____
_____	_____
	_____
_____	_____
	_____

Decision Disaster. Why?

Sally had always been one of the top two students in her small, rural high school. She was delighted when she was accepted by early decision to one of the most selective colleges in the country. In her first semester Sally pulled two D's and failed one course; she was working very hard but had difficulty keeping up with her classmates. She hadn't realized how intense the competition would be at this kind of school.

STEP 6

DESCRIBING THE INFORMATION YOU NEED TO MOVE AHEAD

One gigantic information-gathering task remains—summarizing what you know about the major and most important information categories relating to the college choice. Most students have to know at least some things about these information categories to make a decision. For each college alternative you've been studying, ask yourself, "What do I know and is it enough?" Add new information as you walk through the next steps of your decision.

EXERCISE 16.

WHAT DO I KNOW ABOUT:

College	Admissions Requirements, Standards, and Procedures?	Do I Need More Info?

WHAT DO I KNOW ABOUT:

College	Student Life and Campus Atmosphere	Do I Need More Info?
_____	_____	_____
_____	_____	_____
_____	_____	_____
_____	_____	_____
_____	_____	_____

College	Costs	Do I Need More Info?
_____	_____	_____
_____	_____	_____
_____	_____	_____
_____	_____	_____
_____	_____	_____

College	Financial Aid Opportunities	Do I Need More Info?
_____	_____	_____
_____	_____	_____
_____	_____	_____
_____	_____	_____
_____	_____	_____

WHAT DO I KNOW ABOUT:

College	Athletic and/or Arts Offerings	Do I Need More Info?
_____	_____	_____
_____	_____	_____
_____	_____	_____
_____	_____	_____
_____	_____	_____

College	Academic Requirements	Do I Need More Info?
_____	_____	_____
_____	_____	_____
_____	_____	_____
_____	_____	_____
_____	_____	_____

College	Special Programs (Study Abroad, Independent Study, Career Preparation)	Do I Need More Info?
_____	_____	_____
_____	_____	_____
_____	_____	_____
_____	_____	_____
_____	_____	_____

93

TIME OUT

In identifying the best sources of information, think about things you can read, things you can experience, and people you can talk with. Remember—ask yourself *why* this source would be especially helpful in your response to the questions.

1. What schools have the best or highest percentage of undergraduates going to graduate school?

_____

_____

_____

_____

_____

2. What major gives the best chance of getting a job after graduation?

_____

_____

_____

_____

_____

3. What major insures the best salary upon graduation?

_____

_____

_____

_____

_____

4. Where are the best professors?

_____

_____

_____

_____

_____

5. How can I find out about the best teachers before signing
up for a course?

_____

_____

_____

_____

_____

6. What kind of grading system is there?

_____

_____

_____

_____

_____

7. Where do most of the students come from?

_____

_____

_____

_____

_____

8. What colleges have the best party life?

_____

_____

_____

_____

_____

9. Which colleges are noted for a high degree of school spirit?

_____

_____

_____

_____

_____

10. How available is off-campus housing?

_____

_____

_____

_____

Thought Starter

What kind of information
is most helpful to you when it
comes to determining significant differences among
colleges? What's the best source for this information?

Looking Ahead: Narrowing the Field

You don't want to end up with too many "finalists" (the colleges you intend to apply to) in this decision. You've got to get tough and narrow down the college options that you will consider your final round. While there is no magic number of finalists, if you have more than six you may be spinning your wheels.

In this chapter, you will be concerned with looking ahead. You'll take what you know and focus on the six or so possibilities you feel are the best. To do this, you'll learn a way to reduce your information to three essential questions for eliminating your possibilities. In addition, you'll spend some time thinking about the possible consequences of your choices. We'll begin with a look at consequences first.

Consequences are the things you will have to deal with once you make a decision. Sometimes they can be anticipated, and sometimes they catch you by surprise. When you set out to make a well-considered, well-informed decision, as you have done by working your way through this book, part of your

What Would You Do If . . .

You didn't get into the college of your choice?

You realized you'd have to work full time at least every other year to pay for your college education?

You found the school you chose was a real mistake (after you'd been in attendance for six months)?

Your best friend, with whom you've agreed to go to the same college, didn't get into your top choice college and you did?

You discovered you had real doubts about attending college after high school even though you're a highly qualified student?

Your parents wanted you to go to a college that you didn't like at all?

You were rejected by all the colleges to which you applied?

thinking involves looking ahead and anticipating possible outcomes of your decision. You began this process in Chapter 5 when you identified the outcomes you want from your college experience. In that case, you looked at desirable outcomes specifically. Here we'll try to get you to be alert to the unexpected and the negative as well. It's not possible to avoid negative outcomes entirely, and in any decision of importance you're apt to get a few surprises. The idea is to be prepared! The best way to be prepared? You've guessed it—anticipate the range of possibilities before you make your decision.

As you can see, some of these consequences would have been difficult to avoid unless you had looked into a very special area of college life or collected very detailed information. No matter how conscientious you are in your search for the right college, there will be some missing information.

That's to be expected. However, you can save yourself a few headaches by doing some more anticipating before you make your final decisions. To start the process, in Exercise 17 write down 10 of the very worst outcomes (consequences) that could happen in your college experience. (Don't try to rank the outcomes or to relate them to a college at this point.) Then go back and write down in the second column the information or information source you have that would address the likelihood of each worst outcome occurring.

Thought Starter

Here are a few consequences students have encountered that are surprising and negative:

The work was too difficult.

I didn't like my roommate, and I wasn't allowed to change.

There was no way to make enough money to cover living expenses.

The major I wanted was no longer offered.

I didn't get into the fraternity I wanted.

The coaching staff for minor sports was subpar.

Getting into certain clubs or activities was a matter of who you knew, not qualifications.

Women were clearly second-class citizens.

You couldn't get help when you got into academic difficulty.

There was a tremendous amount of pressure to party.

The career guidance office was of no help in getting jobs.

EXERCISE 17. What's the Worst That Could Happen?

The 10 Worst Outcomes	Information That Would Tell Me the Likelihood of This Happening
1. _____	_____
2. _____	_____
3. _____	_____
4. _____	_____
5. _____	_____
6. _____	_____
7. _____	_____
8. _____	_____
9. _____	_____
10. _____	_____

If you're having trouble getting started, you can use some of the negative outcomes listed in the last Thought Starter. Think, too, about stories you've heard from friends who have had disastrous college experiences. You can even revisit your positive outcomes in Chapter 5 and flip them over on the negative side to enlarge your list.

This isn't an exercise to scare you; it's simply to remind you that anything can happen. And it's one more step toward clarifying the outcomes that speak for or against options you are considering. What you want to do is insure that the colleges you finally apply to have little chance of yielding the kinds of negative outcomes you've identified.

Put together a summary of this information by completing Exercise 18.

EXERCISE 18. Avoiding the Worst Outcomes

This College Option _____

Is Not Likely to Yield This Outcome _____

_____

Because I Know _____

This College Option _____

Is Not Likely to Yield This Outcome _____

_____

Because I Know _____

This College Option _____

Is Not Likely to Yield This Outcome _____

_____

Because I Know _____

This College Option _____

Is Not Likely to Yield This Outcome _____

_____

Because I Know _____

Information Gaps to Fill:

_____

_____

_____

What are three outcomes you *most* want to avoid in your *first* year of college?

1. _____

_____

_____

2. _____

_____

_____

3. _____

_____

_____

There is another outcome it is important to anticipate at this point. That is the outcome or consequence of not getting into the college of your choice. Many of the information resources you have at your disposal can help you predict your chances of gaining admittance to a given college. However, there is no secret mathematical formula that says if you have these kinds of grades, these SAT scores, these achievements, and these special talents you will get into these colleges. Each college uses a slightly different approach, weighs factors differently, and has different people making subjective and objective assessments of applicants. Nevertheless, you will be able to get a general sense of your chances based upon what the colleges say they want, what your guidance counselor knows about you in relation to college criteria, and what you bring to the total picture in terms of unique accomplishments and talents.

In the space below, write down the six or so college options you've chosen. Using what you know now, and adding any information you can find in a directory or college catalog, estimate your chances of being accepted to each (less than 25 percent, less than 50 percent, more than 50 percent, more than 75 percent). Cite specific (key) information that confirms your estimates of probability.

College Option	Chances of Acceptance	Key Information
_____	_____	_____
		_____
_____	_____	_____
		_____
_____	_____	_____
		_____
_____	_____	_____
		_____
_____	_____	_____
		_____
_____	_____	_____
		_____

Are you more confused now than you were when you started? Chances are you're suffering from information overload. Those directories are chock-full of good facts and helpful descriptions of hundreds of colleges, *but*, enough is enough! What you need now is a way to get things focused so you're concentrating your efforts on the information that will make a difference. The process you're about to learn has been designed to fight information overload and, at the same time, to help you focus on the *three* essential questions that must be asked about each of your college options.

Imagine you have in your hands a powerful reduction machine. Instead of reducing humans, it reduces information from the general to the very specific, to a valuable "nugget." The nugget represents a summation of the best pieces of information you have collected to date. Using this machine, you're going to reduce your information from a big, cumbersome boulder to a pure nugget or information gem! All of your information will be processed so that it answers the following three questions with a yes or no.

1. Is my choice realistic in terms of my desired characteristics?
2. Can I win with this choice?
3. Is this choice worth it?

In the following pages you'll discover how to decide which of the percentages of acceptance are OK for you. What's important at this point is that you have started thinking about your admission chances.

TIME OUT

If you had to choose right now, what five options would make the finalist list? Jot down three pieces of information you think are most important for supporting your decisions. Don't forget your Gotta Haves.

The Finalists

Most Important Information That Confirms This College as a Very Likely Choice

_____   _____

_____   _____

_____   _____

_____   _____

_____   _____

In Exercise 19, fill in your lists of Gotta Haves, Like to Haves, and so forth, for all 12 categories. At the top of the columns, write down the names of the colleges you are considering. Then, taking each college one at a time and applying the information you have gathered, answer each of the following questions by placing a +, −, or ? to represent a hit, a miss, or do not know, respectively.

EXERCISE 19. Information Reduction Process

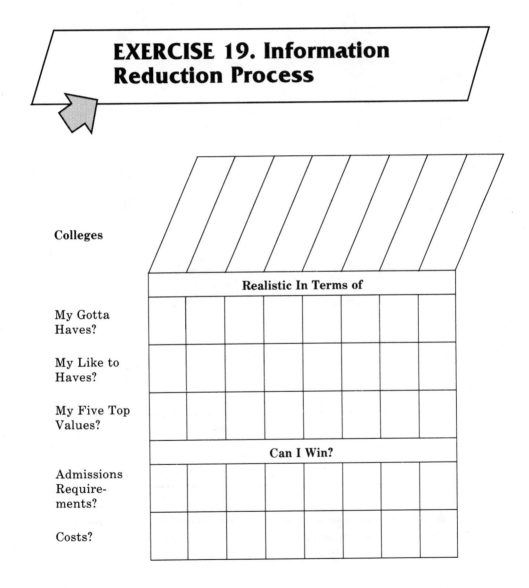

Colleges

	Realistic In Terms of							
My Gotta Haves?								
My Like to Haves?								
My Five Top Values?								
	Can I Win?							
Admissions Requirements?								
Costs?								

Colleges

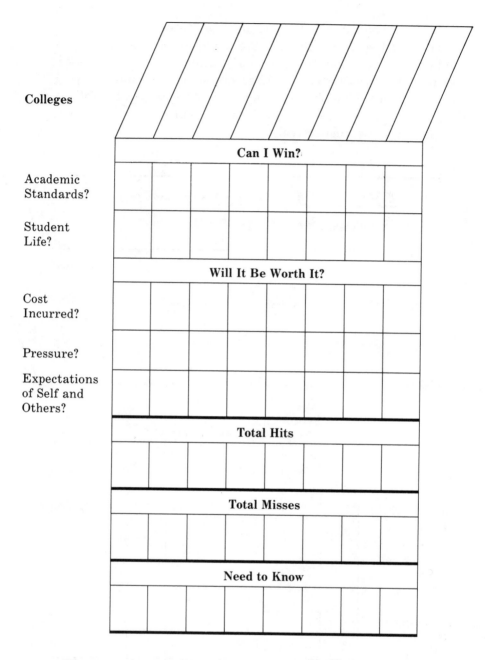

	Can I Win?						

Academic
Standards?

Student
Life?

	Will It Be Worth It?						

Cost
Incurred?

Pressure?

Expectations
of Self and
Others?

	Total Hits						

	Total Misses						

	Need to Know						

When you have tallied the "scores" from your Information Reduction Process worksheet, you should be able to rate each of your college options with a +, −, or ? Do this below.

College Option	Ratings		
	Realistic	Win	Worth It
1. _____	_____	_____	_____
2. _____	_____	_____	_____
3. _____	_____	_____	_____
4. _____	_____	_____	_____
5. _____	_____	_____	_____
6. _____	_____	_____	_____
7. _____	_____	_____	_____
8. _____	_____	_____	_____

The options that receive a hit in all categories will make your final list. If any option has a total of more misses than hits in any of the three major categories, it should probably not be included in your final list.

If you have a lot of need-to-know symbols, you should ask about each one, "Would the answer to this be important in accepting or rejecting a college option?" If you find that the answer is yes, fill in the information gaps before moving to the next stage of this exercise.

Thought Starter

Have you decided the decision you're facing is, "Which colleges are the best for me?" This means you have decided to go to college and not to opt for some other alternative such as work, or work and study, after graduation from high school. Why do you think college is the best after-high-school alternative for you?

Now revisit your list. What option had the most number of hits? The least? Reorder your list so the number one option has the most number of hits and other options are ranked in a descending order from the most to the least number of total hits. Remember, if you have a lot of need-to-knows, do not do your ranking. Fill in those remaining information gaps first.

Your finalist ranking should look like this:

	Total Hits			
Finalist	Realistic	Win	Worth It	Overall
1. _____	_____	_____	_____	_____
2. _____	_____	_____	_____	_____
3. _____	_____	_____	_____	_____
4. _____	_____	_____	_____	_____
5. _____	_____	_____	_____	_____
6. _____	_____	_____	_____	_____
7. _____	_____	_____	_____	_____
8. _____	_____	_____	_____	_____

This ranking does not mean your number one option is your best bet. We'll add in some additional factors in the next chapter relating to risk taking and risk measuring that you'll want to use before you make your final decision.

Learning Summary and Update

To insure your decision has been well considered and well informed to this point and to head off any surprises because you may have missed something important, review the first six steps of the decision process. Write down your answer to each Decision Step question.

Decision Step 1. What priorities and values are you determined to accommodate in your choice? Why?

_____

_____

_____

Decision Step 2. What outcomes do you expect from the college experience? Why?

_____

_____

_____

Decision Step 3. What college options do you know about now?

_____

_____

_____

Decision Step 4. Are there information gaps about these options you need to fill? What are they?

_____

_____

_____

Decision Step 5. How do these options compare with one another? Which emerge as strong possibilities based upon the _realistic, win, worth it_ rating exercise?

_____

_____

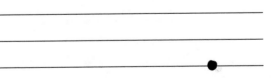

Decision Step 6. Are there any important information gaps you need to address before you can make a final selection? Describe them.

_____

_____

_____

Until you have answered these questions to your satisfaction, there is no need to go on. When you feel you are ready, move to the next chapter and Decision Step 7: Selecting What's Best for You.

TIME OUT

At this point in your decision, what do you feel most apprehensive about? If you could get the answer to three questions, what would those questions be?

1. _____

2. _____

3. _____

Selecting What's Best for You

In many ways, the sky is the limit when you choose a college. Technically, there are no restrictions on your choice except those you impose yourself. When deciding, you'll have to do more than just "add up the numbers." You'll have to factor in your value judgments in terms of the kind of risk you're willing to take. Remember, the selection decision has two parts: first, you identify the most promising and suitable colleges to apply to, and second, you choose among those colleges that actually offer you admission. Depending on the level of risk you are willing to take, the number of colleges offering you admission may be less than the number of applications you file.

The key words in this decision step are "best for you." *Best* means meeting your special needs, goals, dreams, outcomes, and standards. In addition, it means taking what amounts to the best admissions risk. In other words, it means increasing your chances of getting accepted if you do apply. Your task is to figure out your chances as accurately as you can and then to add this information to the other information you have gathered. Study the Best for Me formula.

THE BEST FOR ME FORMULA

Values + Outcomes Desired
+ Characteristics Speaking for
− Characteristics against
− Outcomes to Be Avoided

= The basis for comparing options from the most favorable to the less favorable.

This formula will help you determine your next-to-last ranking of your final options. It is given to get you thinking about what is involved in the selection step of the decision process. Looking at the formula, let's say that your top three options all have about the same standards for admission. You have read the catalogs, checked with your guidance counselor, and visited the three colleges in question. It is clear from these information sources that you have a less than 50 percent chance of getting in. You very much like these three schools, but you're afraid you might be rejected by all three if you do apply. In this case, what risk are you willing to take?

Note that determination of your chances will depend on your individual judgment. There is no mathematical formula and no way to predict your chances with total accuracy. A special talent or accomplishment, an unusual geographic location, or an alumni contact may push you from the reject to the accept category. Since most colleges base their decisions on a variety of factors that each college will weigh differently, it's pretty difficult to be able to say more than "I've got less than 50 percent, better than 50 percent, or about a 75 percent chance of getting in." As you know, some of the most highly qualified students do not get into the college of their choice. So what can you do? It is helpful to formulate a kind of risk strategy that will accommodate a high risk and at the same time protect you from being totally disappointed.

Before you look at these strategies, review what you know now about the admissions risk at each of your college options using the chart on the next two pages.

Once you have put together the information you have about each item, estimate your chances of acceptance for each option using Exercise 20. First, write down your college options in order of preference from your list of finalists in Chapter 8 and indicate the risk under Chances of Acceptance (> 50 percent; < 25 percent, etc.). Then using the Re-rank column, list your options in order of chances of acceptance. Begin with the most likely to accept you as number 1, and so on.

Thought Starter

Take a minute and consider what you would do if...

You were rejected by all the schools to which you applied.

You didn't get into your top three preferences, which you rated far and above any other options.

You were accepted to all the schools to which you applied, but you found out some of your classmates were accepted at more prestigious colleges that you didn't apply to because you felt you had little chance of getting in.

You were accepted to several schools but are not really excited about going to any of them since they were at the bottom of your list.

COLLEGE

Things Read	People Talked To	Other

COLLEGE

Things Read	People Talked To	Other

COLLEGE

Things Read	People Talked To	Other

CHANCES OF ADMISSION ACCORDING TO:

COLLEGE

Things Read	People Talked To	Other

COLLEGE

Things Read	People Talked To	Other

COLLEGE

Things Read	People Talked To	Other

EXERCISE 20. Estimating Your Chances of Getting Accepted

College Options Ranked in Order of Preference	Chances of Acceptance	Re-rank	Key Info
1. _____	_____	_____	_____
2. _____	_____	_____	_____
3. _____	_____	_____	_____
4. _____	_____	_____	_____
5. _____	_____	_____	_____
6. _____	_____	_____	_____
7. _____	_____	_____	_____
8. _____	_____	_____	_____
9. _____	_____	_____	_____
10. _____	_____	_____	_____

This is a rough guess in some ways, but it will begin to highlight the differences between what you prefer and what your chances are of getting it. What was said earlier still holds: You could apply to the colleges of your preference and ignore the risk factor completely. Depending upon your qualifications, this may present little difficulty (you get into all of your choices because you are so highly qualified) or enormous difficulty (you are rejected by all the schools to which you apply).

A more common result of ignoring risk is wasting your time and money by applying to schools that reject you; in the process, you will have ignored those options that would meet your needs more than adequately and that offer a far better chance of acceptance. Now, nobody is suggesting you settle for less than the best. Rather, you want the best for you. This means assessing what you want and what risks you're willing to take to get it.

It all comes down to being able to live with the consequences of the choice you make.

Many students have a hard time living with the consequences of their choices, often because they did not assess risk properly or attempt to prepare for the consequences of the risks they took. You're not going to make the same mistake! For one thing, you've already begun to assess the risk involved in each of your choices. The second thing you'll learn to do is to develop a risk strategy for making your final selections. Developing a strategy involves planning and positioning yourself so you can best attain the results you want. There are three common risk-taking strategies you can use in making your college choice.

Some Risk Strategies You Can Use

Go for It   This strategy is used when you want something very much. So much, you don't care what the chances of getting it are. People who play the lottery use this strategy, as do others who go into business for themselves, which has a success rate of less than 10 percent.

It's OK   This approach is on the safe side. In other words, you are willing to give a little on what is important to you to insure a better chance of getting something that is OK. Not the best, but OK.

No Risk   The message of the No Risk strategy is clear: Avoid risk at all costs! It gives the decider a definite sense of the worst things that could happen and are to be sidestepped by the action taken.

These strategies can be applied to individual college choices and then to the total choice picture. For example, you may find one of your options so appealing you're willing to risk paying an application fee and taking the time to apply even though the chances for acceptance are minimal. However, you may not want to apply this strategy to all choices. An It's OK approach will give you a better chance of getting some of the things you want. Applying this strategy to your overall college choice process, you will most likely avoid being rejected by all your choices. To do this you could select a college or several colleges in the 75 percent chance of acceptance category. If the thing you want to avoid more than anything is total rejection, you should use the No Risk strategy.

While there is no best strategy to cover all situations, your aim will be to get as many acceptances from those schools you think are the best for you and, at the same time, to protect yourself from the worst possible scenario. Sort through your most promising choices and place each under one of the three strategies. Extra space is available to note some other strategy you may wish to apply.

EXERCISE 21. Applying Your Decision Strategy

Go for It	It's OK	No Risk
_____	_____	_____
_____	_____	_____
_____	_____	_____
_____	_____	_____
_____	_____	_____
_____	_____	_____

_____

_____

_____

TIME OUT

Spend a moment looking over your choices. Is there a pretty even distribution among the three columns? Test the risk strategy you've applied by making a brief response to the following:

- Are you sure those options in column one are worth the slim chance they offer? Why?

_____

_____

_____

_____

- Do you have four or more choices in the It's OK column? If so, are you selling yourself short?

_____

_____

_____

_____

- Are you pretty certain to get into one choice listed? Why?

_____

_____

_____

- Do you need to collect some more information about any aspect of your decision before you apply? What remains for you to find out? Why?

_____

_____

- What characteristics in your column one options are worth so much risk on your part? What are the major differences between your column one and column two options other than the chances of admission?

_____

_____

_____

_____

Difficult questions? Sure! They are critical in getting you to fine-tune some of the differences between your options.

There is one major fact to keep in mind. Even if you are rejected by all of your choices on the first go-around, it doesn't mean you will be totally out in the cold. There are opportunities to hook up with a solid college option quite late in the game. We will show you how to deal with this possibility in Chapter 12 when we talk about emergency planning and tactics.

Now you are ready to work through the final exercise of Step 7. It's called the Is It Worth It evaluation. You have identified the things you want and expect from your college choice. You have assessed the chances of getting what you want and have weighed the risk involved against the importance of what you want. As you finalize your choices and select those to which you'll make formal application, you should be able to answer each of these questions in the affirmative for each option. If you can't, then you should take a long look at the particular option and decide whether or not it's worth having on your list.

IS THIS OPTION WORTH IT TO ME?

	Yes	No
Does it accommodate the things important to me to an acceptance level?	____	____
Are my Gotta Haves met by this option?	____	____
Is there a reasonable chance that I will experience the outcomes I want at this college?	____	____
If it didn't turn out right could I survive?	____	____
Is it worth the cost for tuition, etc.?	____	____
Will it adequately prepare me for my future career?	____	____
Will the choice have a positive impact on the people important to me?	____	____

Having screened all your options with the preceding questions, identify the colleges to which you think you will definitely apply. Try working with a list of six. Given all the factors you've utilized in your decision, rate your top choices from one to six. For each choice, give three major reasons for ranking it as you have.

College Option Ranked   **Most Important Reasons for Rank**

#1 _____   1. _____

                              2. _____

                              3. _____

#2 _____   1. _____

                              2. _____

                              3. _____

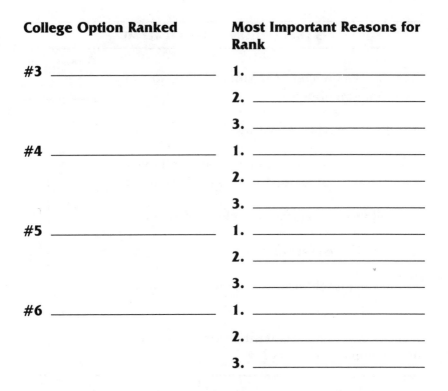

College Option Ranked	Most Important Reasons for Rank
#3 _____	1. _____
	2. _____
	3. _____
#4 _____	1. _____
	2. _____
	3. _____
#5 _____	1. _____
	2. _____
	3. _____
#6 _____	1. _____
	2. _____
	3. _____

Take some time to study this list. These are your finalists, so they should be the best. Check your reasons—do they conform to your values, to your specifications for your ideal college, and do they accommodate your Gotta Haves?

It's a good time to share your thinking with your parents, your college counselor, or both.

CHAPTER

10

Applying for Admission and Financial Aid

You are now in the final drive of the college decision process. Among other things, you have taken or are about to take admissions, achievement, and advanced placement tests; you have narrowed your selections; and you have gathered information by reading catalogs, talking to people, visiting colleges, and conferring with your college counselor and other people interested in your choice. It's time to turn the decisions you've made and the information you've gathered into concrete action.

Is figuring out how to finance your college education a critical part of your decision? You bet! To this point you've done all the legwork and the tough thinking required in making most of the important decisions. To let things slip at this point could negate all the good work you've done. If you follow some of the suggestions below, your Step 8 will be a lot easier and you may actually enjoy the application process.

The first part of Step 8 involves completing the actual application or form for admission. The second part will address applying for financial help. You'll want to read the financial section even if you think you do not need or are not eligible for assistance.

Your application can be an important part, even the turning point, of an admissions decision. To be sure that you prepare the best possible applications, follow the steps below carefully.

1. Read the application thoroughly. Do not complete any portion until you have read it.
2. Fill in the informational items first. It's best to do this on a blank sheet of paper before you write or type on the application form itself.
3. Save the essay and your record of achievements and other accomplishments for last.
4. Complete the Uniqueness Profile and Proud Accomplishments exercises on the following page before completing the essay and accomplishment portion.
5. Write the essay on a blank sheet of paper and give it a good proofreading to check for mistakes. Get reactions and suggestions from other people before you record the final essay.
6. Review all material for mistakes, omissions, etc.

The next series of activities has been designed to help you focus on the things that may make a difference in your essay. Colleges do pay attention to how you approach the essay. You might view it as an opportunity to show how you are unique or special in some way. In short, you're trying to get the college to "buy" you, or more specifically, to perceive you as an important asset they would like to have at their institution. As you might imagine, most colleges are going to read thousands of essays ranging from the straightforward to literary abstractions, and from the modest to sheer puffery.

Common sense suggests that your essay be clear, accurate, to the point, and shorter rather than longer. It needs to convey that you have done some thinking about the focus of your essay and that you are able to go beyond the obvious. Most essay portions of the application leave room for creativity as long as your presentation is clear. Unfortunately, many students waste a lot of time on the essay portion of the application because they leap before they think. This ready, fire, aim approach is exactly what you do not want. So, before you get to it take a few minutes to think!

Before attempting to complete your essay, work through the following exercises.

EXERCISE 22. Your Uniqueness Profile

When writing your application essay, the idea is to put your best foot forward, to show that you are special. Everybody has something special or unique about them, but sometimes we are not able to see our own uniqueness because we take ourselves for granted.

This exercise will help you to identify your own special and unique qualities and experiences. On the worksheet, write down for each category one or two things (interests, skills, and so forth) that you feel best represent you. Then write down what each reveals about you and also the limitations each might imply.

After you have filled in all the categories, ask for feedback from friends, teachers, parents, your college counselor, and others who know you well.

	Uniqueness category	What this reveals about you	Limitations spotted
Interests:			
Special Skills:			
Experiences of Note:			
Paid and Unpaid Work:			

	Uniqueness category	What this reveals about you	Limitations spotted
Special Personal Qualities:			
Aptitudes:			
Attitudes:			
Other:			

Once you have completed your uniqueness profile, look again at each category and identify a specific accomplishment or other evidence that demonstrates your unique interest, skills, etc. For example, your love for sports might have led you to form a community team for younger kids, to do an exposé of illegal high school residences allowing certain schools to have ineligible players, or to ride the bench for three years as an enthusiastic team member of limited talent.

EXERCISE 23.

Write down at least one accomplishment or piece of evidence for each category below.

Uniqueness Accomplishment/Evidence Summary:

Interests: _____

_____

_____

Special Skills: _____

_____

_____

Experiences: _____

_____

_____

Work: _____

_____

_____

Personal Qualities: _____

_____

_____

Aptitudes: _____

_____

_____

Attitudes: _____

_____

_____

Another approach to demonstrating your "specialness" is to explain why you think you are capable of doing or achieving what you say you can do. It's called *probing for credibility* since your credibility is what you are trying to prove, in part, to anybody who reads your college application. This process begins with identifying one accomplishment of which you are especially proud. It could be anything from being the first in your family to complete high school to winning a national competition in mathematics. The trick is to be able to describe this accomplishment in detail from beginning to end. If you can describe what you have done in detail, others will find it more believable that you'll be able to repeat a similar accomplishment in the future!

EXERCISE 24. Your Proud Accomplishments

Pick three things you have done over the past two years of which you are especially proud and write them below.

1. _____

2. _____

3. _____

Now select one of the above accomplishments and explain in detail, from beginning to end, exactly what you had to do in order to achieve it. Remember, this is what *you* did:

_____

_____

_____

_____

_____

_____

What did this accomplishment reveal about you? Your values, likes, weaknesses, and so forth?

_____

_____

_____

_____

_____

Now you have two sources of information pointing to your uniqueness. Put them together and extract those things that show you in your best light. Read the essay requirements on the applications of each college to which you are applying. Make a list of those highlights you want to incorporate into each essay. Again, get feedback from at least one other person before you actually begin writing the essays.

In some cases, you may not be able to capture in writing the things that best demonstrate your uniqueness. In these cases, you may wish to forward examples of your creative writing, artwork, photography, and so forth, which need to be seen in order to be fully understood. This is perfectly OK as long as you don't overburden the admissions people with too much supportive material. Sometimes supportive material can serve to balance other information. For example, a modest SAT score might be helped by a creative writing sample.

However, remember that the essay is still one of the most important parts of the application. As you begin writing, keep the following Dos and Don'ts in mind:

- Think before you write.
- Keep things neat. Check in advance for spelling and omissions.
- Don't exceed the space allotted on the application.
- Be concise and clear. Make your point!
- Emphasize a strong commitment you've made to something.
- List your most important accomplishments first.
- Tie your activities to the themes running through your essay.
- Be accurate!
- Ask yourself, "What will make this college remember me?"
- Review your completed application, *carefully.*

EXERCISE 25. Planning Your Essay

Options	Essay Requirements	What You'll Include as Your Highlights
#1 _____	_____	_____
	_____	_____
	_____	_____

Options	Essay Requirements	What You'll Include as Your Highlights
#2 _____	_____	_____
	_____	_____
	_____	_____
#3 _____	_____	_____
	_____	_____
	_____	_____

Money Matters—How To Apply

Most colleges suggest a "financial blind" approach to making an application. In other words, you should submit an application to all the colleges you are interested in before you worry about the cost of each. This is good in theory, but in reality it seems foolish to pay to apply to a school you could not afford to attend. The one thing you can count on is that college will be expensive—more expensive than the published suggested budgets for colleges indicate. There is no question that some highly qualified students will not be able to attend their college of preference because of lack of money.

Earlier in the book you addressed some of the risk factors relating to admissions, and it was suggested that all applicants ask the question, "Is it worth it?" This is especially true when the cost of college is a consideration of prime importance to you. There are no easy ways to determine if the cost of something is worth it. You will have to make a personal value judgment, usually combined with input from your family.

While the bad news is that costs of education are high, the good news is that there are many creative ways to finance your education. Colleges tend to be quite flexible when it comes to allowing you some leeway to pay for your education. In addition, some of the most expensive colleges have the most money available for financial aid.

To determine what the policies and procedures relating to financial aid are for each of your college choices, make your first step a call to each financial aid office or a review of the section on financial aid in each college catalog. From both sources, you will find out about required forms, application deadlines, and the types of aid available.

In most applications for financial aid, you will have to fill out a form (usually with the help of and supporting documentation from your parents or guardian). One such form, the Financial Aid Form (FAF), is a need analysis that your parents will complete and send off to be processed. Your financial "need" will then be forwarded to those colleges you have designated. Colleges do their best to meet your verified need, but they may not be able to meet it in full. Most likely, you'll be expected to earn some money during the summer or nonschool months and perhaps to accept some form of work-study during the school year, in addition to any grants, loans, or scholarships you have accepted.

The Financial Aid Form will give you some good rule-of-thumb expectations in its guidelines for estimating your financial need based upon family income, assets, number of children in school, and so forth. Some of the guidebooks listed in the reference section will be useful as well. With the tuition and room and board at some colleges getting close to $20,000, most families will require some kind of financial aid.

To begin the financial application process it is useful to estimate the total yearly cost of attending each college. The college catalogs and guidebooks will give you an idea as to room and board, tuition, fees, and books for a year. Some will even project an annual expense budget. To play it safe, add 2 to 5 percent to any budget you develop or read about; this will cover any "extra" and unpredictable costs you might encounter during the typical college year.

Try the following exercise. Refer to the information you have gathered and estimate an annual budget for three of your top choices using the categories suggested.

EXERCISE 26. Estimated Annual College Budget

Category	College 1	College 2	College 3
Tuition	————	————	————
Fees	————	————	————
Room	————	————	————
Board	————	————	————
Books	————	————	————
Laundry	————	————	————
Travel	————	————	————
Recreation/social	————	————	————
Clothes	————	————	————
Extra food	————	————	————
Subtotal	————	————	————
Times 2%-5%	————	————	————
Total Estimated Expenses	————	————	————

Paying the Bills

With your budgets in hand, sit down with your parents (if you expect them to help you with your college costs) and ask them how much they will be able to contribute toward your college expenses each year. Then estimate how much (if any) work income you plan to earn and contribute each year.

On the following worksheet, subtract these two amounts and any savings you might have from the total expenses you estimated on your budgets. The amounts remaining will have to be funded by financial aid or other sources.

EXPENSE CONTRIBUTION WORKSHEET

	College 1	College 2	College 3
Total Estimated Expenses	_____	_____	_____
Less: Family Contribution	_____	_____	_____
Part-Time Work Income	_____	_____	_____
Personal Savings	_____	_____	_____
Total Remaining Expenses	_____	_____	_____

In addition to applying for financial aid, it is important to develop different strategies for paying for college. Here are some alternatives:

Part-Time Work: You can find jobs on campus or start your own business, such as running deliveries, laundry, typing, tutoring.

Work-Study: Some colleges offer work and study combinations.

Work/Alternative Year: It is usually acceptable to request a year or half year off to make money. As a student in good standing, you may find this a viable alternative and also not a bad thing to have on your résumé.

Transfer: State and two-year schools tend to be a lot less expensive than private colleges.

Transfer (continued)   Two years at a less expensive school and a final two years at a more expensive college may meet your financial needs and still give you a degree from a school that may have been your first choice except for the cost.

If applicable, investigate the policies on the above options at each of the schools to which you are considering applying. In any case, do not prematurely give up on your preferred choices because of the financial picture. Get out there and do a lot of digging first.

You may also find that once you begin your college experience you'll get a lot of fresh ideas about how students pay for their education. In addition, if you are a student in good standing, college counselors are in a better position to help you put together a plan for meeting your needs. It may take more than four years, but you have lots of time. A year or two of work in order to "pay" for the best possible education will be rewarding in the long term.

Review these words of advice and caution before you move on:

- Check all deadlines for applying for aid, which vary from college to college. If you're late you probably will hurt your chances.
- Don't rely on the college to meet your financial need. Check the financial guidebooks and research all the grants and scholarships that are available to students at local, state, and national levels.
- All work and no play can make you a pretty unhappy person. You may be willing to earn money in every spare moment, but be sure to allow some time to enjoy the uniqueness of your college years. To work more than 15 hours a week is probably pushing it.
- Don't assume you and your family are not eligible for assistance of some sort. Parent loans are available to people at virtually all income levels.

- The best aid package in terms of amount may not be the best for you. Consider the short- and long-term implications of the aid package for you and your family.
- Colleges, even private colleges, have a wide range of costs. There are some good "buys" all around. In most cases, you'll have to find them through a directory or guidebook.
- Don't be unreasonably swayed by the prestige or so-called status colleges. There are many fine state institutions, which will cost a lot less. How much is status worth? That depends on what's important to you and what the long-term payout is likely to be.
- Don't overlook the obvious. Your college counselor probably has some good information about local resources and previous student experiences; this may be more useful to you than the most comprehensive book on financial aid.
- Don't delay! Begin researching financial aid options early in your junior year.
- Things change. Make sure your information is up to date. Procedures and rules for aid change all the time. For the latest information, it's best to speak with the financial aid officer at each of the colleges of your choice.

TIME OUT

Write down all the advantages you might realize by working your way through college over a six-year period.

_____

_____

_____

_____

_____

_____

What are the disadvantages?

_____

_____

_____

_____

_____

_____

_____

_____

Decision Disaster. Why?

Ingrid stopped exploring certain college options whenever the tuition and fees went over a certain figure. Many of her classmates were accepted to colleges she would have liked to have attended if she could have afforded it. Ingrid wondered if she had settled for less than the best.

They Decide,
You Decide

Once those applications have been submitted, your work for the moment is pretty much done. You'll feel some relief, but it won't last long. This is suspense time. Lots of waiting and wondering. Just about every day somebody will be sharing some news about a college, an acceptance, a rejection, or whatever. It's a time when you'll probably wonder why you didn't try early decision. Then you'd be able to avoid all the waiting. Furthermore, you know the decision is in the hands of somebody else and in a process that is not even close to being perfect. Add to this the second thoughts about your final applications—all those things you forgot to say—and it's easy to understand why many students think this is the worst part of the whole admissions process!

Since things are pretty much out of your control at this point, accept that fact. Relax! Enjoy your senior year for the next couple of months. The real nail-biting time isn't going to come until late March or April. When it does come, you'll be back in control. It will be your turn to decide!

A lot can happen from the time you apply to the time you actually receive the decisions from the various colleges. You might have found additional information, good or bad, about the colleges to which you applied. You may have developed some new interests or priorities that will have an impact on your final choice, or perhaps your family's financial situation has changed in some way.

In any case, close to the time of receiving your admissions decisions (say, February or early March), review and update the criteria you used to narrow your choices by working through the following exercise. Write down any new ideas or concerns or objectives you have regarding the college experience for each of the following categories:

EXERCISE 27. What's New or Different about . . .

My college objectives: _____

_____

_____

The importance of certain college characteristics: _____

_____

_____

My interests: _____

_____

_____

My relationships: _____

_____

_____

My family finances: _____

_____

My career plans: _____

_____

_____

_____

Other: _____

_____

_____

What impact might this new information have on my college decision?

_____

_____

What action should I take prior to receiving acceptances and/ or rejections?

_____

_____

_____

_____

_____

_____

_____

_____

_____

You will find this updated information useful when you make your final enrollment decision. Are you ready for the next step?

STEP 9

One of the ironies of this stage of the admissions process is that your decision will be a difficult one whether you are accepted by most of your preferred choices or rejected by most of them. Both situations will require a full application of the decision process you worked through in previous chapters. About the only time this part of the process is easy is when you are absolutely clear about your first choice and have been accepted, or when you have only a single option remaining because the news has not been good. In the vast majority of situations, you'll be forced to look at your remaining alternatives and to compare them carefully before you make your choice.

Let's take a look at a number of application decisions colleges might make, including:

Acceptance or acceptance with conditions (You need to take a writing skills course prior to enrolling.)

Acceptance delayed (You are in but you have to start in February, not in September.)

Wait list (It's not a no, but it may be far from a yes.)

Rejection (No question here.)

Regardless of the response you get, you'll have decisions to make.

Depending on what strategy you used in making your selections, you may find you have no acceptances in hand or that the one or two acceptances you do have are so unappealing that you have little or no desire to pursue them. If this has happened to you, we will show you how to deal with this in the next chapter.

You may find that you have been wait-listed by one of your top options. What does this mean? The wait list is used by colleges for different reasons. Sometimes it is a courtesy extended to special-status students, such as children of alumni who are simply not qualified but are offered a place on the wait list to soften the blow of outright rejection. In other cases, it is a kind of safety valve that enables the college to go to the wait list if not as many students enroll as anticipated. Thus, the college will fill the empty spots using people on the wait list. In some cases, it may mean that you were a close call and with a little extra push you might make it. The wait list has a wide range of meanings, and you don't want to waste time waiting to hear which meaning applies to you. It is possible and very important to clarify what your wait list decision means. Sometimes a college counselor can find out, and sometimes you can get the information from the person at the college who interviewed you or from an alumnus who supported your application. The key questions are: What is my status? Is it worth doing something about?

Here are some moves to consider if you are put on the wait list:

- Don't pursue the wait list unless this is a very important option for you.
- Find out what it means in your case.
- Get support for your application. An additional word or two from a teacher, counselor, or alumnus can help.
- Write a letter telling the college you will attend if accepted.
- Send along any new information you did not have at the time of application.

Wait list or no, you're back in the decision mode. You're now going to make a commitment to enroll in a single college—a choice that is not cut-and-dried by any means. Chances are you have a number of positive options that are very close in terms of their appeal.

We'll proceed with the notion that you will have some options, whether you're thrilled about them or not.

EXERCISE 28. Updating Your Decision

The first thing you'll want to do is revisit your lists of Gotta, Like To, and Must Not Haves in Chapter 5. You might also want to look at your Ideal College exercise in Chapter 6 and your Realistic, Win, Worth It answers in Chapter 8. Compare these to your current thoughts in the What's New or Different exercise you just completed. Can you think of anything else that has changed for you?

_____

_____

_____

_____

_____

Additions: _____

_____

_____

_____

_____

Keeping the above exercises and updates in mind, you are now ready for the home stretch!

On a blank sheet of paper, copy the grid on the next page as many times as you have acceptances (or wait lists). Fill in one grid per college, listing the strengths, weaknesses, opportunities, and problems that each offers. Remember to use the probing _why_. Why is this feature a strength? Why might this aspect present a problem? Then below each grid write down the outcomes you expect from each college experience and also any final information gaps you may have uncovered.

COLLEGE OPTION:

Strengths	Weaknesses

Opportunities	Problem(s)

Outcomes I Can Expect	Information Gap

When you have completed all your grids, compare them. Which is the strongest; which offers the most opportunities? If there is important information you still need to gather, do this before proceeding (if there is time). In the space below, rank your final three top choices. As a safety measure, spell out your rationale for each ranking. Also be sure to note any potential problems you might encounter at each of your top choices. By doing this in advance, you can begin to prepare for and possibly minimize or avoid the problems.

RANKING YOUR FINAL OPTIONS

OPTION #1

Major Reasons for Attending	Possible Problems

OPTION #2

Major Reasons for Attending	Possible Problems

OPTION #3

Major Reasons for Attending	Possible Problems

Thought Starter

Many students feel
these are the most important
questions to address when making their final decision.
Have you considered them in making your choice?

Is there a specific degree program that I want? _____

_____

Will the social life meet my needs? _____

_____

_____

_____

_____

How far in miles/travel time do I want to be from home?

_____

_____

Can my interests be met in a small town/big city/country environment? _____

_____

_____

_____

_____

If I don't like the school, will the credits be recognized by other colleges? _____

_____

_____

By now, you should be ready, even eager, to make your choice. Soon you'll be stepping into a very different environment that will have significant impact on your life in both the short and the long term. If you have worked through all the decision process exercises in this book, you should be on your way to an exciting, enjoyable, and worthwhile experience. Enjoy!

When Things
Don't Work Out

There's always the chance things will not turn out the way
you want them to. That's true about anything in life, and
that is precisely why the last step focuses on contingency
planning or What Ifs. If in fact you've found that the remaining options or lack of them puts you in what appears to be an
impossible situation, you'll want to think about alternative
tactics for getting what you want.

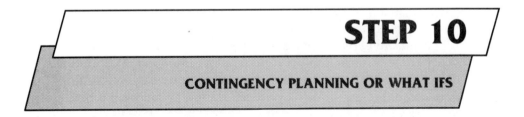

STEP 10

CONTINGENCY PLANNING OR WHAT IFS

There are three situations thousands of students face each
year when they receive their college admissions decisions.
These are:

149

No acceptances

Acceptances from not very acceptable colleges

Not enough money to attend the colleges that are acceptable

None of the above situations is the end of the world for anybody. You may feel that way for a while. You are likely to be pretty down when you find out most people are happy with their options and that you are the exception. Just as with any disappointment, you'll have a choice to make: give up in anger or despair, or take charge and turn your situation around. Let's look at each situation separately and generate some ideas about what could be done *if* this should happen to you!

No Acceptances

This is pretty rare because most students apply to at least one or two schools they are pretty sure about. But a few students apply only to equally difficult alternatives, and come up empty-handed. Others make poor decisions in the first place and are bound to be disappointed. Your first step in this situation is to try to find out why you were not accepted. Confer with your college counselor. If going to college, any college, is your number one priority, then you have several strategies to consider.

First, with the help of your counselor, identify local two- and four-year colleges that have relatively open admission requirements. Visit these schools in person, and bring along your decision criteria so you can ask the questions that will give you the information you want.

Second, investigate more selective colleges that will permit you to attend part-time as a nonmatriculated student. If you do opt for this status, you may be able to "prove" yourself and gain regular acceptance by attaining a certain grade point average in a given number of courses. This tactic puts you in college right away, even if it is only part-time.

Third, each year some colleges of good quality do have room for last-minute applications. From year to year they contact high schools to let them know there is space available. Check again with your college counselor.

Finally, although it may take a little more time, consider addressing your weaknesses by taking some skill-building courses or by enrolling in another school for another year of high school. While it might take longer it may, in the long run, get you the acceptance you always wanted. An extra year of school can add enormously to your qualifications and maturity.

The Unacceptable Acceptances

In this situation, you have to be really careful. You might be playing some early mind games with yourself. After all, if you did go through the decision process how could the remaining options be unacceptable? Ask yourself the following questions: Am I reacting with a bruised ego? Am I feeling a bit sorry for myself because my friends got into more prestigious schools? Or am I really faced with some options that I simply can't or wouldn't feel right about pursuing? To find out where you stand, write down the answers to the following questions:

What's unacceptable about this option? _____

_____

_____

Why are these things unacceptable? _____

_____

_____

_____

What would make it more acceptable? _____

_____

_____

_____

Can I live with it for one year? Two? _____

_____

_____

What's the single biggest concern I have about this college?

_____

_____

Once you have worked through these questions, turn the exercise around. Jot down all the aspects of this option that you feel you could live with. You'll probably have several entries for each category.

THINGS I COULD LIVE WITH

Academic Program _____

_____

Social Life _____

_____

Location _____

_____

Cost _____

_____

Preparation for the Future _____

_____

If there are one or two factors that might make this option more acceptable or unacceptable, pursue them by collecting more information or by discussing your concerns with your parents, teachers, or college counselor. A visit to the college itself would be useful and appropriate. Remember, no choice is final. You can always transfer, drop out, join the service, or pursue some of those options suggested above to the student who received _no_ acceptances.

Interview at least two college graduates who have been working three or more years and three recent college graduates. Get at least one new idea from each as to how you can earn money while attending college. Make sure their suggestions are specific. Traditional college aid sources such as grants, scholarships, and work-study are *not* new ideas.

NEW IDEAS

1. _____

2. _____

3. _____

4. _____

5. _____

6. _____

When the Money Just Isn't There

The high cost of college is enough to scare anybody. However, the long-term payoff (college graduates will end up earning far more than high school graduates) demands that you not toss in the towel too quickly. You're not the first person who has been disappointed, even resentful, to find that lack of money could wipe away the value of your achievements, preventing your access to the college of your choice. But now that you have the bad news, let's look at some encouraging words.

If you have been accepted to a college you really want to attend but simply cannot afford, contact the college immediately. If you can, arrange to visit the admissions and financial aid offices. There just might be something extra floating around in the way of aid that you don't know about. If there isn't, ask about your options. Is it possible to delay admission for six months or a year? Is it likely more aid will be available later in the year? Will you get the same aid package if you delay your admission six months? Answers to these questions will buy you some time to put together additional resources or to investigate new financial aid possibilities.

You might have to consider some combination of part-time job and college. Another option is military service, which provides some nice educational as well as financial benefits. It is also possible to alternate a year of work with a year of college until you obtain your degree.

If at all possible, it is worth while to follow the foot-in-the-door strategy. Once you are enrolled you are apt to become much more aware of the many ways to earn money on campus. The following exercise will show you how to uncover some of these opportunities in advance.

Stepping into
Your Future—
The Opportunity

You can do just about anything as long as you value it enough and plan for it. The world after high school is full of different kinds of decisions, often in a very different setting. You'll be exposed to a wide variety of people, multiple course offerings, new relationships, different value systems, and a great many very talented people who are going to test your mettle.

It has been said that change is a pain as well as an opportunity, and this is worth thinking about. Change is a deviation from experience, and this means leaving some of your comfort zones to tackle new things you might not be instantly successful with. Given this situation, many students fight to stay with what they do well and are reluctant to seize the opportunities that exist all around them when they get to college. As a result, many students can look back on the experience with some regret. They simply would not let go of those "safe" and comfortable habits.

The opportunity is there, and you'll enjoy pursuing some of the options that will stretch you and help you grow as a person. College is a great chance to explore, to discover, and to reevaluate what is really important to you in life. Pass-fail marking systems, as well as other "nongraded" course options, provide an excellent way to venture into something new without a great deal of risk.

In many ways, you have one of the rare chances in life to try out some things, to make a mistake and not be penalized for it. College is all about growth and learning and gaining confidence. You'll get much more out of it than you put in, but your effort will have a lot to do with how you feel four years later and whether you'll be proud or regretful about the things you did or did not do. When awards are handed out at graduation or when you attempt to write a summary of your four years for your yearbook, you'll get a clear and revealing sense of the kind of effort you made over the four years.

Once again, it's a matter of taking full advantage of your resources—the faculty, students, social life, athletics, special trips, and off-campus work or internship opportunities. And don't forget to take a look at yourself along the way. You'll change and so will your needs and priorities. Some students outgrow their colleges in two years and others never do feel they are in the best place for them. Both situations require action. It's perfectly OK to go through your decision process again. It would be a mistake simply to continue on the same course even after you realized the "fit" was not a good one for you.

Remember, you have made this decision. Therefore you are responsible for it and for any consequences—good and bad— that evolve. You can be sure things won't always be perfect— far from it! You may get a problem roommate. You may flunk your first paper or test. Perhaps you won't make the fraternity or sorority you wanted or maybe your closest friend will get into another relationship and you'll suddenly feel very much alone. Anything can happen and you need to be prepared for it.

As you begin this very special experience, keep your eyes open. Learn as much about your new college, "your home away from home," as quickly as you can. Confer with others but do your own thinking. Remember, all good decisions depend upon an accurate assessment of you and what is important to you. With this in mind you might observe these guidelines for a successful experience:

Be yourself. Faking it isn't worth the effort and you'll be found out anyway.

Reassess. Take a fresh look at the experience after six months and then after a year. Is the college still living up to your expectations? Are there any disappointments? Why?

Plan. Plans give you focus and reduce surprise. By planning ahead you'll have the best chance to get the courses you want, the professor who is best, or even a place to live off-campus that is desirable.

Use resources. Ask questions. Talk to your instructors. Clarify, clarify, and clarify more. People want to help you. Ask for help.

Set goals. Establish a target each semester relating to something personal or something that will show up in your college performance.

Take a risk. Once a year do something that will make you stretch beyond your comfort areas. Work on a weakness.

Take action. If you want something, go after it. People can't read your mind. Let others know what you're feeling and why.

Get to know others. Go beyond your immediate circle of friends. Every new acquaintance has the potential to add to your learning in some special way.

Avoid second-hand opinions. Get your information directly. Don't be put off by an opinion that could have impact for you. Check it out!

And remember. No decision is totally final. If things don't work out you can just revisit the decision process you have utilized in this book. And if things do work out well, before long you'll be applying this process to your after-college choice and to other future decisions. You now have a best and helpful friend—a process for making a well-considered choice anytime and anywhere!

Resources and References

While no attempt is made here to supply an exhaustive list of information resources to help you with your choice, some suggestions are made that will get you moving in the right direction. Your guidance office will have some of these references, as will your local library. More important than the information itself is your approach. You want to make sure you know the kind of information you need and why. Otherwise, you'll soon be afflicted with a severe case of information overload that will leave you frustrated and anxious and not much closer to a better decision.

Let's see if you've really done some thinking about the resources that will help you make a better decision. Listed below in several categories are some of the things you can do to expand your information about college. See if you are able to think up other resources that might prove helpful under each category.

INFORMATION RESOURCES

People to Talk With | **Information They Might Supply**

College Counselor _____

Parents _____

Alumni _____

College students _____

Financial aid officer _____

People to Talk With	Information They Might Supply
Admissions director at a college	_____
A person in a career of interest to you	_____

Experiences	How Would This Help With My Decision?
A campus visit	_____
Taking an Advanced Placement course	_____
Living away from home for a month	_____
Doing an independent study project	_____
Running for class office	_____
Working part-time in an office	_____
Interviewing adults in different careers	_____

Things to Read	What Would I Want to Find Out? Be Specific!
A college catalog	_____
The Yellow Pages	_____
A handbook on all colleges	_____
A book about choosing a career	_____
A college yearbook	_____
A college newspaper	_____

Things to Think About	What Would be Helpful About This? Why?
My dreams	_____
Career goals	_____
People I like to be with	_____
Where I'd like to be in five years	_____
Things I don't enjoy doing	_____

REFERENCES

Career Planning

Bureau of Labor Statistics, U.S. Department of Labor. *Occupational Outlook Handbook.* Washington, D.C.: U.S. Government Printing Office. Annual.

Mitchell, Joyce Slayton. *The College Board Guide to Jobs and Career Planning.* New York: College Entrance Examination Board. Available in July 1990.

Financing College

Adams, Janelle P., editor. *The A's and B's of Academic Scholarships.* 12th edition. Alexandria, Va.: Octameron, 1990.

The American Legion. *Need a Lift?* Indianapolis: The American Legion, National Emblem Sales. Annual.

The College Board. *The College Cost Book.* New York: College Entrance Examination Board. Annual.

U.S. Department of Education. *The Student Guide: Five Federal Financial Aid Programs.* Washington, D.C.: U.S. Government Printing Office, 1989.

Time Management

Eisenberg, Ronni, and Kate Kelly. *Organizing Yourself.* New York: Macmillan, 1986.

Haynes, Marion E. *Personal Time Management*. Los Altos, Calif.: Crisp, 1987.

Lakein, Alan. *How to Get Control of Your Time and Your Life*. New York: McKay, 1973.

Schneider, Zola Dincin, and Phyllis B. Kalb. *Countdown to College: Every Student's Guide to Getting the Most Out of High School*. New York: College Entrance Examination Board, 1989.

Index

Academic requirements, analysis of, 93

Acceptance decision
with conditions, 142
contingency planning for, 149–154
enrollment choice and, 142–148
lack of acceptances, 150–151
unacceptable acceptances, 151–152

Accomplishments, analysis of, 124, 128–130

Action and control stage of decision making, 13–14, 27, 29, 123–161
applying for admission in, 123–131
applying for financial aid in, 132–138
contingency planning in, 149–154
continued growth in, 155–158
enrollment choice and, 142–148
re-analysis of expectations in, 140–141, 147–148

Admissions offices, 71, 160

Admissions requirements
analysis of, 91, 103–105, 111–115
delayed admission, 135, 154
essay in, 124–125, 130–131
financial aid application, 63, 132–138
preparing applications to meet, 123–131
Proud Accomplishments and, 124, 128–130
risk strategy and, 117–120
Uniqueness Profile and, 124, 125–128

Admissions standards, 91

Advanced Placement courses, 160

Alternative development stage of decision making, 13, 27, 29, 55–96
comparing alternatives and outcomes in, 84–90
identifying known alternatives in, 66–77
identifying new alternatives in, 77–82
information resources for, 63, 70–77, 82, 91–96, 159–161
personal priorities in, 59–64
specifications for colleges in, 56–58

Alumni, 159

Aptitudes, analysis of, 127

Arts programs, analysis of, 93

Athletic programs, analysis of, 93

Attitudes, analysis of, 127. See also Self-analysis; Values

Budgets, estimated annual, 133–134

Campus atmosphere, analysis of, 92, 96

Campus trips, 71, 74, 92, 96, 160

Career preparation, 93, 94

College catalogs, 63, 70, 103, 160

College counselors, 2, 71, 74, 136, 137, 159

College directories, 70, 74, 103, 160

College fairs, 71

College Handbook, The, 63

College selection. See Selection stage of decision making

College students, as information source, 71, 159

Contingency planning, 149–154
for financial aid problems, 153–154
for no acceptances, 150–151
for unacceptable acceptances, 151–152

Control stage of decision making. See Action and control stage of decision making

Costs, analysis of, 92, 105, 106, 132–134

Counselors, 2, 71, 74, 136, 137, 159

Deadlines, 136

Decision making, 11–24
action and control stage of. See Action and control stage of decision making
alternative development stage of. See Alternative development stage of decision making
analysis of types of, 6

Decision making *(continued)*
  by college, 142–143
  contingency planning and, 149–154
  continued re-evaluation in, 140–141, 155–158
  developing a personal history of, 14–24
  expectations and, 48–54
  Identification stage of. *See* Identification stage of decision making
  living with decisions in, 117
  nature of a decision in, 11–13
  objective of, 12
  sample plan for, 29
  selection stage of. *See* Selection stage of decision making
  self-analysis and. *See* Self-analysis; Values
  stages of, 13–14, 27, 29
Delayed admission, 135, 154

Early decision, 28, 139
Essay, 124–125, 130–131
Expectations, 48–54
  and college choice, 157
  comparing alternatives and outcomes, 84–90
  guidelines for developing, 50–51
  methods of analyzing, 52–54
  in rating college options, 78–82
  typical set of, for college, 49
Experiences, analysis of notable, 126

Financial aid, 63, 132–138
  analysis of opportunities for, 92
  cost of college and, 132–134
  Financial Aid Form (FAF), 132–133
  problems in obtaining, 153–154
Financial Aid Form (FAF), 132–133
Financial aid officers, 71, 137, 159
Friends, 2, 71

Goals, 157
Grading systems, 57, 95, 156
Grants, 133, 136
Guidance counselors, 2, 71, 74, 136, 137, 159

Housing, 57, 96, 160

Ideal college, description of, 67–71
Identification stage of decision making, 13, 26–27, 29, 31–54
  analysis of expectations in, 48–54
  analysis of values in, 32–38
  marketing your value profile in, 39–45
  value conflicts in, 37–38, 41–48
Independent study programs, 71, 93, 160
Influencers, and college choice, 2, 5–9
Information Power Chart, 87–90
Information resources, 82
  analyzing need for additional, 84–96
  campus trips, 71, 74, 92, 96, 160
  college catalogs, 63, 70, 103, 160
  college directories, 70, 74, 103, 160
  college students, 71, 159
  counselors, 2, 71, 74, 136, 137, 159
  financial aid officers, 71, 137, 159
  identifying best, 94–96
  identifying new, 72–77
  lists of, 70–71, 159–161
Interests, analysis of personal, 126

Loans, 133
  to parents, 136

Majors, 94
Measurement, of objectives, 50
Military service, 154

New courses, 75
Newspapers, college, 160
Nongraded courses, 156

Objectives
  guidelines for developing, 50–51
  methods of analyzing, 52–54
  typical college, 49
  updating personal, 140–141
  See also Self-analysis; Values
Opinions, 157
Outcomes
  analysis of potential worst, 100–104
  comparing alternatives and, 84–90

Parents, 2, 8, 71, 159
  and financial aid, 132–135
  loans to, 136
Part-time work, 126, 133–135, 154, 160
  advantages and disadvantages of, 137–138
  amount of, 136
Pass-fail systems, 156
Personal qualities, analysis of, 127
Planning
  contingency, 149–154
  for essay, 130–131
  importance of continued, 157
  for information gathering, 71–76
  problems of, 2
  stages of, 26–29
Priorities. *See* Self-analysis; Values
Professors, analysis of, 58, 95
Proud Accomplishments, list of, 124, 128–130

Rejection decision, 142, 143, 149–152
Relevance, of objectives, 51
Risks
  analysis of, 23–24
  and the college experience, 155–158
  developing strategy for handling, 117–120
Roommates, 61

Scheduling
  for decision making, 29
  of objectives, 51
Scholarships, 133, 136
School spirit, 96
Selection stage of decision making, 13, 27, 29, 97–122
  chances of admission in, 112–118
  enrollment choice and, 142–148
  influences on, 2, 5–9
  potential worst outcomes in, 100–104
  rating options in, 78–82, 104–110, 121–122, 146
  strategy for, 118–122
Self-analysis, 31–54, 161
  decision-making forces and, 46–48
  expectations and, 48–54
  exploring alternatives in, 66–82

influences on college choice, 2, 5–9, 142–148
  as information resource, 71
  of likes and dislikes, 22–23
  marketing with your values, 39–45
  personal history of decision making in, 14–18
  of personal values, 32–38
  in setting college specifications, 56–64
  situational analysis in, 19–21
  updating personal objectives, 140–141
  See also Values
Situational analysis, 19–21
Special programs, analysis of, 93
Special skills, analysis of, 126
Specifications, in college selection, 56–64
  Gotta Haves, 59–61, 63
  Like to Haves, 59–61, 63
  Must Haves, 62
Status, importance of, 137
Student life, analysis of, 92, 96, 106
Study abroad, 93

Teachers, 2, 71
Transfer students, 135
Travel, away from home, 7, 71, 160

Uniqueness Profile, 124, 125–128

Values
  in analysis of alternatives and outcomes, 87–90
  analysis of personal, 32–38
  conflicts in, 37–38, 41–48
  decision making and, 32–48, 111–113
  expectations and, 48–54
  personal marketing based on, 39–45
  in rating college options, 78–82
  in setting college specifications, 56–64
  See also Self-analysis

Wait list decision, 142–143
Work/alternative year, 135, 154
Work-study programs, 133–135

Yearbooks, college, 160

165

Other Books of Interest from the College Board

**Item
Number**

003179   *Campus Health Guide*, by Carol L. Otis, M.D., and Roger Goldingay. A comprehensive medical guide, written expressly for college students, that stresses the link between a healthy lifestyle and a productive college experience. ISBN: 0-87447-317-9, $14.95

.002601   *Campus Visits and College Interviews*, by Zola Dincin Schneider. An "insider's" guide to campus visits and college interviews, including 12 checklists that will help students make the most of these firsthand opportunities. ISBN: 0-87447-260-1, $9.95

002261   *The College Admissions Organizer.* This unique planning tool for college-bound students includes inserts and fill-in forms, plus 12 large pockets to store important admissions materials. ISBN: 0-87447-226-1, $16.95

002687   *The College Board Achievement Tests.* Complete and actual Achievement Tests given in 13 subjects, plus the College Board's official advice on taking the tests. ISBN: 0-87447-268-7, $9.95

003101   *The College Board Guide to Preparing for the PSAT/NMSQT* Contains four actual tests as well as practical test-taking tips, sample questions, and a comprehensive math review section. ISBN: 0-87447-310-1, $8.95

002938   *The College Board Guide to the CLEP Examinations.* Contains nearly 900 questions from CLEP general and subject examinations, plus other information. ISBN: 0-87447-293-8, $8.95

003047   *College Bound: The Student's Handbook for Getting Ready, Moving In, and Succeeding on Campus*, by Evelyn Kaye and Janet Gardner. Help for high school seniors as they face the responsibilities and independence of being college freshmen. ISBN: 0-87447-304-7, $9.95

003381   *The College Cost Book, 1989-90.* A step-by-step guide to 1988–89 college costs and detailed financial aid for 3,100 accredited institutions. ISBN: 0-87447-338-1, $13.95 (Updated annually)

003160   *The College Guide for Parents*, by Charles J. Shields. Useful information on such topics as college choice, standardized testing, college applications, financial aid, and coping with separation anxiety. ISBN: 0-87447-316-0, $12.95

003365   *The College Handbook, 1989-90.* The College Board's official directory to more than 3,100 two- and four-year colleges and universities. ISBN: 0-87447-336-5, $17.95 (Updated annually)

002490   *College to Career*, by Joyce Slayton Mitchell. A guide to more than 100 careers, telling what the work is like, the education and personal skills needed, how many people are employed, where they work, and starting salaries and future employment prospects. ISBN: 0-87447-249-0, $9.95

003349   *Coping with Stress in College*, by Mark Rowh. The first book to examine the stresses specifically related to college life, this provides students with practical advice and guidelines for coping with stress. ISBN: 0-87447-334-9, $9.95

003357   *Countdown to College: Every Student's Guide to Getting the Most Out of High School*, by Zola Dincin Schneider and Phyllis B. Kalb. A one-of-a-kind book to help every teenager do well in high school and be prepared for college. ISBN: 0-87447-335-7, $9.95.

003055   *How to ⌐elp Your Teenager Find the Right Career*, by Charles J. Shields. Step-by-step advice and innovative ideas to help parents motivate their children to explore careers and find alternatives suited to their interests and abilities. ISBN: 0-87447-305-5, $12.95

002482   *How to Pay for Your Children's College Education*, by Gerald Krefetz. Practical advice to help parents of high school students, as well as of young children, finance their children's college education. ISBN: 0-87447-248-2, $12.95

003373   *Index of Majors, 1989-90*. Lists over 500 majors at the 3,000 colleges and graduate institutions, state by state, that offer them. ISBN: 0-87447-337-3, $14.95 (Updated annually)

002911   *Profiles in Achievement*, by Charles M. Holloway. Traces the careers of eight outstanding men and women who used education as the key to later success. (Hardcover, ISBN: 0-87447-291-1, $15.95); 002857 paperback (ISBN: 0-87447-285-7, $9.95)

003535   *The Student's Guide to Good Writing*, by Rick Dalton and Marianne Dalton. Guidelines and detailed information on how to meet the challenges of writing assignments for *all* college courses. ISBN: 0-87447-353-5, $9.95

002598   *Succeed with Math*, by Sheila Tobias. A *practical* guide that helps students overcome math anxiety and gives them the tools for mastering the subject in high school and college courses as well as the world of work. ISBN: 0-87447-259-8, $12.95

003225   *Summer on Campus*, by Shirley Levin. A comprehensive guide to more than 250 summer programs at over 150 universities. ISBN: 0-87447-322-5, $9.95

003039   *10 SATs: Third Edition*. Ten actual, recently administered SATs plus the full text of *Taking the SAT*, the College Board's official advice. ISBN: 0-87447-303-9, $9.95

002571   *Writing Your College Application Essay*, by Sarah Myers McGinty. An informative and reassuring book that helps students write distinctive application essays and explains what colleges are looking for in these essays. ISBN: 0-87447-257-1, $9.95

002474   *Your College Application*, by Scott Gelband, Catherine Kubale, and Eric Schorr. A step-by-step guide to help students do their best on college applications. ISBN: 0-87447-247-4, $9.95

To order by direct mail any books not available in your local bookstore, please specify the item number and send your request with a check made payable to the College Board for the full amount to: College Board Publications, Department M53, Box 886, New York, New York 10101-0886. Allow 30 days for delivery. An institutional purchase order is required in order to be billed, and postage will be charged on all billed orders. Telephone orders are not accepted, but information regarding any of the above titles is available by calling Publications Customer Service at (212) 713-8165.